FREE DVD  FREE DVD

From Stress to Success DVD from Trivium Test Prep

Dear Customer,

Thank you for purchasing from Trivium Test Prep! We're honored to help you prepare for your HESI A² exam.

To show our appreciation, we're offering a **FREE *HESI A² Essential Test Tips* Video by Trivium Test Prep**.* Our video includes 35 test preparation strategies that will make you successful on the HESI. All we ask is that you email us your feedback and describe your experience with our product. Amazing, awful, or just so-so: we want to hear what you have to say!

To receive your **FREE *HESI A² Essential Test Tips* Video**, please email us at 5star@ triviumtestprep.com. Include "Free 5 Star" in the subject line and the following information in your email:

1. The title of the product you purchased.
2. Your rating from 1 – 5 (with 5 being the best).
3. Your feedback about the product, including how our materials helped you meet your goals and ways in which we can improve our products.
4. Your full name and shipping address so we can send your **FREE *HESI A² Essential Test Tips* Video**.

If you have any questions or concerns please feel free to contact us directly at 5star@trivium-testprep.com.

Thank you!

- Trivium Test Prep Team

*To get access to the free video please email us at 5star@triviumtestprep.com, and please follow the instructions above.

HESI A^2 PRACTICE TEST QUESTIONS 2022-2023:

350+ Practice Questions for the HESI Admission Assessment Exam

Elissa Simon

TABLE OF CONTENTS

WANT MORE?

Try our online *HESI A² Prep Course*

Dear Reader,

Here at Trivium Test Prep, we understand how important scoring well on the HESI A² exam is for your future. We believe you can never be "too prepared" for such a life-changing test. We are excited to offer you a comprehensive online course devoted to the HESI A²! Our ***HESI A² Prep Course*** includes:

- a <u>complete review</u> of all content on the HESI A² exam, with **trackable course progress** so you know exactly what you still need to review;
- <u>subject quizzes</u> at the end of each section, so you can **assess your retention** before moving on to new units;
- <u>two full practice exams</u> with **fully explained answer rationales** and **trackable scoring**, so you can measure your progress and understand what you need to improve on;
- and <u>full accessibility</u> via your computer, tablet, and mobile phone 24/7, enabling you to **learn at home or on-the-go!**

Best of all, our unique material and practice questions are available exclusively through ***HESI A² Prep Course***, ensuring you get double the study time when coupled with this book!

Trivium Test Prep's ***HESI A² Prep Course*** is available to current customers like you at the promotional price of only **$39.99!** Many less convenient programs retail for hundreds of dollars online. To enroll today and start learning immediately, please visit:

http://course.triviumtestprep.com/

Thank you for choosing Trivium Test Prep for all your HESI A² study needs! Best of luck with your studies,

— *The Trivium Test Prep Team*

INTRODUCTION

Congratulations on your decision to join the field of nursing—few other professions are so rewarding! By purchasing this book, you've already taken the first step toward succeeding in your career. The next step is to do well on the HESI Admission Assessment (HESI A²) exam, which will require you to demonstrate knowledge of high-school level reading, writing, math, and science.

This book will walk you through the important concepts in each of these subjects and also provide you with insider information on test strategies and tactics. Even if it's been years since you graduated from high school or cracked open a textbook, don't worry—this book contains everything you'll need for the HESI A².

WHAT'S ON THE TEST?

The HESI A² is an eight-section, computer-based exam. Different schools will require different sections as part of their applications, so you'll want to make sure you know what sections you need to take on test day.

You can work through the sections on the HESI A² in any order, so you should plan in advance how you'd like to tackle the test. Some students like to start with the section they find the hardest, while others like to focus their efforts on sections they know they'll do well on. The time limits listed below are recommendations by the administrators of the HESI A² exam. You do not need to strictly adhere to these suggestions, but these limits may be helpful as you practice pacing yourself for other board certification exams.

1. **Mathematics: 55 questions, 50 minutes**

   The Mathematics section of the HESI A² focuses on skills required for health care professionals. You will see questions on basic addition, subtraction, multiplication, and division. You will also need to have knowledge of roman numerals, calculating dosages, measurements, fractions, and proportions.

2. **Reading: 55 questions, 60 minutes**

   The Reading section assesses your ability to read, analyze, and comprehend short passages related to health and medicine. You will need to be able to identify the main idea of a passage, make inferences about that passage, and interpret information in the passage from context clues.

3. **Vocabulary: 55 questions, 50 minutes**

   You will be tested on your knowledge of words, specifically those relating to the health field (although not all questions will be health related).

4. **Grammar: 55 questions, 50 minutes**

   The Grammar section will test your knowledge of basic grammar, parts of speech, common grammatical errors, and sentence structure.

5. **Biology: 30 questions, 25 minutes**

   The Biology section covers topics such as cellular respiration, photosynthesis, genetics, biological molecules, and cells. This, and the other science sections, can be tricky because there are only thirty questions that cover a wide range of material.

6. **Chemistry: 30 questions, 25 minutes**

   The Chemistry section covers topics such as the periodic table, chemical equations, atomic structure, chemical bonding, nuclear chemistry, and chemical reactions.

7. **Anatomy and Physiology: 30 questions, 25 minutes**

   The Anatomy and Physiology section covers a wide spectrum of body systems, including the muscular, skeletal, nervous, renal/urinary, reproductive, endocrine, circulatory, and respiratory systems.

8. **Physics: 30 questions, 25 minutes**

   Very few test takers will actually have the physics section on their exam, as this is excluded by many colleges. If you do encounter it, you will be tested on mechanics, energy, forces, waves, and light. Even if you do have this section on your test, do not focus your efforts here, as mathematics and the other sciences are typically much more important.

   Other Unscored Sections

   You may also encounter other unscored sections on the HESI A^2 called *learner profile* exams. These exams will not be used as part of your score. Instead, they are designed to help students better understand their strengths and weaknesses, learning styles and habits, and other personality traits.

Each scored section on the HESI A^2 includes five pilot questions that are not scored. These questions are used by the writers of the HESI A^2 to test new material and will not count toward your final score. However, you won't know which questions these are as you're taking the test, so treat every question like it counts.

HOW IS THE HESI A^2 SCORED?

You cannot "pass" or "fail" the HESI A^2. Your score is simply indicative of your current level of comprehension. However, each school has its own entrance requirements, so check the requirements of the institutions that you want to attend. Also, each institution has different requirements regarding the sections of the test you will take; make sure to check that you're taking the proper exam before you spend your time studying for a subject that you won't necessarily need.

HOW DOES THIS BOOK WORK?

The questions in this book are divided into a review of the general topics covered on the exam. This is not intended to cover everything you'll see on the test: there is no way to cram all of that material into one book! Instead, we are going to help you practice the questions you're likely to see on the test. With time, practice, and determination, you'll be well-prepared for test day.

Now that you have a firm understanding of the exam and what is included our book, don't forget that learning how to study, as well as how to successfully pass an exam, is just as important as the content. Trivium Test Prep would like to remind you as you begin your studies that we are offering a **FREE *From Stress to Success* DVD**. Our DVD includes 35 test preparation strategies that will help keep you calm and collected before and during your big exam. All we ask is that you email us your feedback and describe your experience with our product. Amazing, awful, or just so-so: we want to hear what you have to say!

To receive your **FREE *From Stress to Success* DVD**, please email us at 5star@triviumtestprep.com. Include

"Free 5 Star" in the subject line and the following information in your email:

1. The title of the product you purchased.
2. Your rating from 1 – 5 (with 5 being the best).
3. Your feedback about the product, including how our materials helped you meet your goals and ways in which we can improve our products.
4. Your full name and shipping address so we can send your **FREE *From Stress to Success* DVD**.

TEST YOUR KNOWLEDGE

MATHEMATICS

Directions: Read the problem carefully, and choose the best answer.

1. A car dealership's commercials claim that this year's models are 20% off the list price, plus they will pay the first 3 monthly payments. If a car is listed for $26,580, and the monthly payments are set at $250, which of the following is the total potential savings?

A) $1,282

B) $5,566

C) $6,066

D) $20,514

2. A dry cleaner charges $3 per shirt, $6 per pair of pants, and an extra $5 per item for mending. Annie drops off 5 shirts and 4 pairs of pants, 2 of which need mending. Assuming the cleaner charges an 8% sales tax, which of the following will be the amount of Annie's total bill?

A) $45.08

B) $49.00

C) $52.92

D) $88.20

3. A sandwich shop earns $4 for every sandwich (*s*) it sells, $2 for every drink (*d*), and $1 for every cookie (*c*). If this is all the shop sells, which of the following equations represents what the shop's revenue (*r*) is over three days?

A) $r = 4s + 2d + 1c$

B) $r = 8s + 4d + 2c$

C) $r = 12s + 6d + 3c$

D) $r = 16s + 8d + 4c$

4. Which of the following is the *y*-intercept of the line whose equation is $7y - 42x + 7 = 0$?

A) $\left(\frac{1}{6}, 0\right)$

B) $(6, 0)$

C) $(0, -1)$

D) $(-1, 0)$

5. $4 - \frac{1}{2^2} + 24 \div (8 + 12)$

Simplify the expression. Which of the following is correct?

A) 1.39

B) 2.74

C) 4.95

D) 15.28

6. A rectangular field has area of 1452 square feet. If the width is three times greater than the length, which of the following is the length of the field?

A) 22 feet

B) 44 feet

C) 242 feet

D) 1452 feet

7. The owner of a newspaper has noticed that print subscriptions have gone down 40% while online subscriptions have gone up 60%. Print subscriptions once accounted for 70% of the newspaper's business, and online subscriptions accounted for 25%. Which of the following is the overall percentage growth or decline in business?

A) 13% decline

B) 15% decline

C) 28% growth

D) Business has stayed the same.

8. $(6.4)(2.8) \div 0.4$

Simplify the expression. Which of the following is correct?

A) 16.62

B) 17.92

C) 41.55

D) 44.80

9. Bridget is repainting her rectangular bedroom. Two walls measure 15 feet by 9 feet, and the other two measure 12.5 feet by 9 feet. One gallon of paint covers an average of 32 square meters. Which of the following is the number of gallons of paint that Bridget will use? (There are 3.28 feet in 1 meter.)

A) 0.72 gallons

B) 1.43 gallons

C) 4.72 gallons

D) 15.5 gallons

10. $5\frac{2}{3} \times 1\frac{7}{8} \div \frac{1}{3}$

Simplify the expression. Which of the following is correct?

A. $3\frac{13}{24}$

B. $6\frac{3}{4}$

C. $15\frac{3}{4}$

D. $31\frac{7}{8}$

11. Based on a favorable performance review at work, Matt receives a $\frac{3}{20}$ increase in his hourly wage. If his original hourly wage is represented by w, which of the following represents his new wage?

A) $0.15w$

B) $0.85w$

C) $1.12w$

D) $1.15w$

12. A restaurant employs servers, hosts, and managers in a ratio of 9:2:1. If there are 36 total employees, which of the following is the number of hosts at the restaurant?

A) 3

B) 4

C) 6

D) 8

13. If x is the proportion of men who play an instrument, y is the proportion of women who play an instrument, and z is the total number of men, which of the following is true?

A. $\frac{z}{x}$ = number of men who play an instrument

B. $(1 - z)x$ = number of men who do not play an instrument

C. $(1 - x)z$ = number of men who do not play an instrument

D. $(1 - y)z$ = number of women who do not play an instrument

14. A woman's dinner bill comes to $48.30. If she adds a 20% tip, which of the following will be her total bill?

   A) $9.66

   B) $38.64

   C) $48.30

   D) $57.96

15. Which of the following lists is in order from least to greatest?

   A) $\frac{1}{7}$, 0.125, $\frac{6}{9}$, 0.60

   B) $\frac{1}{7}$, 0.125, 0.60, $\frac{6}{9}$

   C) 0.125, $\frac{1}{7}$, 0.60, $\frac{6}{9}$

   D) 0.125, $\frac{1}{7}$, 0.125, $\frac{6}{9}$, 0.60

16. Which of the following is equivalent to 3.28?

   A) $3\frac{1}{50}$

   B) $3\frac{1}{25}$

   C) $3\frac{7}{50}$

   D) $3\frac{7}{25}$

17. $x \div 7 = x - 36$

   Solve the equation. Which of the following is correct?

   A) $x = 6$

   B) $x = 42$

   C) $x = 126$

   D) $x = 252$

18. After taxes, a worker earned $15,036 in 7 months. Which of the following is the amount the worker earned in 2 months?

   A) $2,148

   B) $4,296

   C) $6,444

   D) $8,592

19. If m represents a car's average mileage in miles per gallon, p represents the price of gas in dollars per gallon, and d represents a distance in miles, which of the following algebraic equations represents the cost c of gas per mile?

   A) $c = \frac{dp}{m}$

   B) $c = \frac{p}{m}$

   C) $c = \frac{mp}{d}$

   D) $c = \frac{m}{p}$

20. Melissa is ordering fencing to enclose a square area of 5625 square feet. Which of the following is the number of feet of fencing she needs?

   A) 75 feet

   B) 150 feet

   C) 300 feet

   D) 5,625 feet

21. Adam is painting the outside of a 4-walled shed. The shed is 5 feet wide, 4 feet deep, and 7 feet high. Which of the following is the amount of paint Adam will need for the four walls?

   A) 80 ft.^{2}

   B) 126 ft.^{2}

   C) 140 ft.^{2}

   D) 560 ft.^{2}

22. A circular swimming pool has a circumference of 49 feet. Which of the following is the diameter of the pool?

   A) 15.6 feet

   B) 17.8 feet

   C) 49 feet

   D) 153.9 feet

CONTINUE

23. Table 1.1. Employee Hours

EMPLOYEE	HOURS WORKED
Suzanne	42
Joe	38
Mark	25
Ellen	50
Jill	45
Rob	46
Nicole	17
Deb	41

The table above shows the number of hours worked by employees during the week. Which of the following is the median number of hours worked per week by the employees?

A) 38

B) 41

C) 42

D) 41.5

24. According to the graph, which of the following was Sam's average monthly income from January through May? (Round to the nearest hundred.)

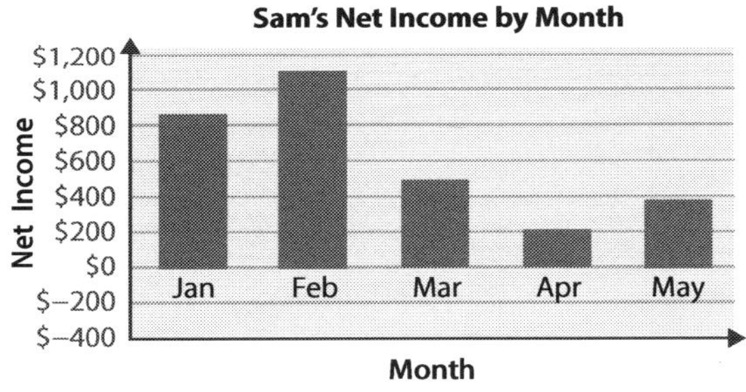

A) $200

B) $500

C) $600

D) $1,100

25. Which of the following is equivalent to 8 pounds and 8 ounces? (Round to the nearest tenth of a kilogram.)

A) 3.6 kilograms

B) 3.9 kilograms

C) 17.6 kilograms

D) 18.7 kilograms

26. $(4.71 \times 10^3) - (2.98 \times 10^2)$

Simplify the expression. Which of the following is correct?

A) 1.73×10

B) 4.412×10^2

C) 1.73×10^3

D) 4.412×10^3

27. Which of the following is not a negative value?

A) $(-3)(-1)(2)(-1)$

B) $14 - 7 + (-7)$

C) $7 - 10 + (-8)$

D) $-5(-2)(-3)$

28. $10^2 - 7(3 - 4) - 25$

Simplify the expression. Which of the following is correct?

A) -12

B) 2

C) 68

D) 82

29. $\dfrac{5^2(3) + 3(-2)^2}{4 + 3^2 - 2(5 - 8)}$

Simplify the expression. Which of the following is correct?

A) $\dfrac{9}{8}$

B) $\dfrac{87}{19}$

C) 9

D) $\dfrac{21}{2}$

30. Anna is buying fruit at the farmers' market. She selects 1.2 kilograms of apples, 800 grams of bananas, and 300 grams of strawberries. The farmer charges her a flat rate of $4 per kilogram. Which of the following is the total cost of her produce?

A) $4.40

B) $5.24

C) $9.20

D) $48.80

31. $\left(1\frac{1}{2}\right)\left(2\frac{2}{3}\right) \div 1\frac{1}{4}$

Simplify the expression. Which of the following is correct?

A) $3\frac{1}{12}$

B) $3\frac{1}{5}$

C) 4

D) 5

32. Which of the following lists is in order from least to greatest?

A) $2^{-1}, -\frac{4}{3}, (-1)^3, \frac{2}{5}$

B) $-\frac{4}{3}, (-1)^3, 2^{-1}, \frac{2}{5}$

C) $-\frac{4}{3}, \frac{2}{5}, 2^{-1}, (-1)^3$

D) $-\frac{4}{3}, (-1)^3, \frac{2}{5}, 2^{-1}$

33. Which of the following is 2.7834 rounded to the nearest tenth?

A) 2.7

B) 2.78

C) 2.8

D) 2.88

34. $\dfrac{4x - 5}{3} = \dfrac{\frac{1}{2}(2x - 6)}{5}$

Simplify the expression. Which of the following is the value of x?

A) $-\frac{2}{7}$

B) $-\frac{4}{17}$

C) $\frac{16}{17}$

D) $\frac{8}{7}$

35. $8x - 6 = 3x + 24$

Solve the equation. Which of the following is correct?

A) $x = 2.5$

B) $x = 3.6$

C) $x = 5$

D) $x = 6$

36. A student gets 42 questions out of 48 correct on a quiz. Which of the following is the percentage of questions that the student answered correctly?

A) 1.14%

B) 82.50%

C) 85.00%

D) 87.50%

37. $4x \div (x - 1)$

Which of the following is the value of the expression above when $x = 5$?

A) 0

B) 1

C) 4

D) 5

38. Which of the following is the slope of the graph below?

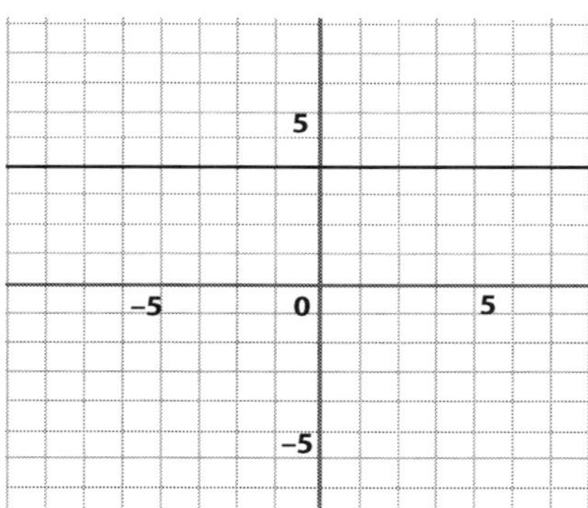

A) ∞

B) non-existent

C) 0

D) 1

CONTINUE

39. Alex, David, and Rachel go out to dinner. Alex and David decide to split an appetizer that costs $8.50, and Rachel gets her own appetizer that costs $6.50. Rachel orders lemonade that costs $3, while Alex and David drink the free water. They all order entrées that cost the same price. They split up the bill according to what each person ordered. Which of the following states how much less Alex and David will pay than Rachel?

A) $1.00

B) $5.00

C) $5.25

D) $7.25

40. There are 450 students in the tenth grade. Of these, 46% are boys. If 21% of the girls have already turned 16, which of the following is the number of girls in the tenth grade who are 16?

A) 43

B) 51

C) 54

D) 94

41. A faucet is leaking 1 drop every 4 seconds. If 1 gallon is equal to 15,140 drops, which of the following lengths of time will it take for this faucet to leak 1 gallon of water?

A) 1 hour, 3 minutes, 5 seconds

B) 4 hours, 12 minutes, 20 seconds

C) 16 hours, 49 minutes, 20 seconds

D) 18 hours, 24 minutes, 5 seconds

42. $(3 + 5)^2 + 24 \div 16 - 5 \div 2$

Simplify the expression. Which of the following is correct?

A) 0.25

B) 30.25

C) 33

D) 63

43. Ashley has been training for a 10-kilometer race. Her average training pace is 8 minutes and 15 seconds per mile. If she maintains this pace during the race, which of the following will be her finishing time? (1 mile = 5280 feet; 1 foot = 0.3048 meters)

A) 51:23

B) 50:53

C) 51:14

D) 82:30

44. $\dfrac{8}{15} \div \dfrac{1}{6}$

Simplify the expression. Which of the following is correct?

A) $3\dfrac{1}{15}$

B) $\dfrac{15}{48}$

C) $\dfrac{4}{45}$

D) $3\dfrac{1}{5}$

45. A marinade recipe calls for 2 tablespoons of lemon juice for $\dfrac{1}{4}$ cup of olive oil. Which of the following is the amount of lemon juice that should be used with $\dfrac{2}{3}$ cup olive oil?

A) $5\dfrac{1}{3}$ tbsp.

B) $\dfrac{3}{4}$ tbsp.

C) 4 tbsp.

D) $2\dfrac{1}{3}$ tbsp.

46. If x represents the proportion of ninth graders in a particular school who are female, and y represents the proportion of students in the school who are ninth graders, which of the following is the expression for the proportion of students in the school who are female ninth graders?

A) $x + y$

B) $\dfrac{x}{y}$

C) xy

D) $\dfrac{y}{x}$

47. Toledo has been working full time but would like to cut back to part time. He normally works from 9:00 a.m. to 5:00 p.m. Monday through Friday. Now he leaves at 1:00 p.m. on Tuesdays and Thursdays. Which of the following is the percentage by which he decreased his weekly work hours?

A) 20%

B) 25%

C) 30%

D) 80%

48. Which of the following lists is in order from least to greatest?

A) $\frac{1}{24} < \frac{3}{32} < \frac{5}{48} < \frac{2}{16} < \frac{3}{16}$

B) $\frac{1}{24} < \frac{5}{48} < \frac{3}{32} < \frac{2}{16} < \frac{3}{16}$

C) $\frac{1}{24} < \frac{3}{32} < \frac{2}{16} < \frac{3}{16} < \frac{5}{48}$

D) $\frac{1}{24} < \frac{2}{16} < \frac{3}{32} < \frac{3}{16} < \frac{5}{48}$

49. $3a + 4 = 2a$

Solve the equation. Which of the following is correct?

A) $a = -4$

B) $a = 4$

C) $a = \frac{-4}{5}$

D) $a = \frac{4}{5}$

50. Caroline reads 40 pages in 45 minutes. Which of the following is the approximate number minutes it will take her to read 265 pages?

A) 202 minutes

B) 236 minutes

C) 265 minutes

D) 298 minutes

51. Jane earns $15 per hour babysitting. If she starts out with $275 in her bank account, which of the following equations represents the amount of hours she will need to spend babysitting in order for her account to reach $400?

A) $275 = 400 + 15h$

B) $400 = 15h$

C) $400 = \frac{15}{h} + 275$

D) $400 = 275 + 15h$

52. Which of the following is the total surface area of a box that is 12 inches long, 18 inches wide, and 6 inches high?

A) 144 sq. in.

B) 396 sq. in.

C) 792 sq. in.

D) 1,296 cu. in.

53. Which of the following has the greatest numeric value?

A) $-4(3)(-2)$

B) $-16 - 17 + 31$

C) $18 - 15 + 27$

D) $-20 + 10 + 10$

54. A pizza has a diameter of 10 inches. If a slice with a central angle of 40 degrees is cut from the pizza, which of the following will be the surface area of the pizza slice?

A) 9.2. sq. in.

B) 8.7 sq. in.

C) 3.5 sq. in.

D) 17.4 sq. in.

55. Meg rolled a 6-sided die 4 times, and her first 3 rolls were 1, 3, and 5. If the average of the 4 rolls is 2.5, which of the following was the value of the 4th roll?

A) 1

B) 2

C) 3

D) 5

56. The data set below shows the number of instruments played by students in the seventh and tenth grades. Which of the following is the difference in the average number of instruments played by seventh- and tenth-graders?

Table 1.2. Instruments Played

STUDENT	GRADE	NUMBER OF INSTRUMENTS
Alison	7	2
Dana	10	0
Jerry	7	1
Sam	7	1
Luke	10	1
Philip	7	2
Briana	10	1
Laura	10	0
Angie	7	2

A) 0.5

B) 1

C) 1.1

D) 2.1

57. If there are 3.28 feet in 1 meter, which of the following is equivalent to 55 meters? (Round to the nearest tenth.)

A) 16.8 feet

B) 21.7 feet

C) 139.7 feet

D) 180.4 feet

58. $-(3)^2 + (5 - 7)^2 - 3(4 - 8)$

Simplify the expression. Which of the following is correct?

A) -17

B) -1

C) 7

D) 25

59. The pie chart below shows a high school graduating class' enrollment in 4 types of universities: small private, large private, small public, and large public. Of the students who enrolled in a public university, which of the following is the percentage enrolled in a small public university?

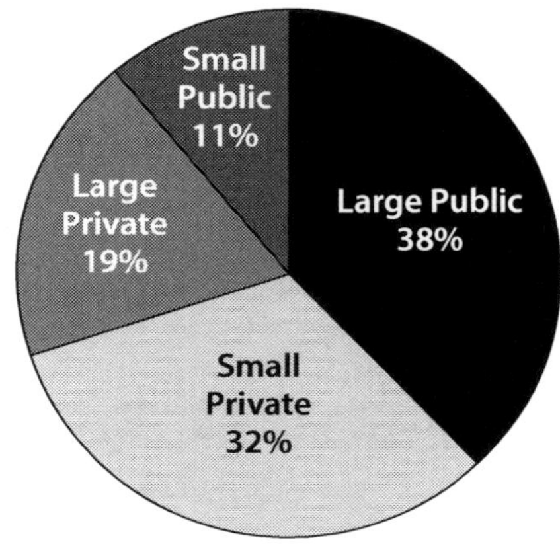

A) 11%

B) 22%

C) 27%

D) 29%

60. $(3^2 \div 1^3) - (4 - 8^2) + 2^4$

Simplify the expression. Which of the following is correct?

A) -35

B) -4

C) 28

D) 85

61. $17.38 - 19.26 + 14.2$

Simplify the expression. Which of the following is correct?

A) 12.08

B) 12.32

C) 16.08

D) 16.22

62. A cylindrical canister is 9 inches high and has a diameter of 5 inches. The formula for the volume of a cylinder is $V = \pi r^2 h$ where r is the radius and h is the height. Which of the following is the volume of the canister?

A) 176.6 in^2

B) 45 in^2

C) 141.4 in^2

D) 706.9 in^2

63. $\dfrac{7}{8} - \dfrac{1}{10} - \dfrac{2}{3}$

Simplify the expression. Which of the following is correct?

A) $\dfrac{1}{30}$

B) $\dfrac{13}{120}$

C) $\dfrac{4}{21}$

D) $\dfrac{4}{105}$

64. Which of the following is equivalent to $4\frac{10}{11}$?

A) 4.09

B) $4.\overline{09}$

C) 4.90

D) $4.\overline{90}$

65. Which of the following shows 74,365 rounded to the nearest hundred and to the nearest thousand?

A) hundred: 74,400; thousand: 74,000

B) hundred: 74,300; thousand: 75,000

C) hundred: 74,400; thousand: 75,000

D) hundred: 74,300; thousand: 74,000

66. A store recorded the following sales over one week:

Table 1.3. Recorded Sales

DAY	SALES
Monday	$300
Tuesday	$250
Wednesday	$550
Thursday	$475
Friday	$325
Saturday	$800

Which of the following is the ratio of the highest amount of sales to total sales for the week and the ratio of lowest amount of sales to total sales for the week?

A) lowest: $\dfrac{13}{108}$; highest: $\dfrac{8}{27}$

B) lowest: $\dfrac{13}{108}$; highest: $\dfrac{11}{54}$

C) lowest: $\dfrac{5}{54}$; highest: $\dfrac{8}{27}$

D) lowest: $\dfrac{5}{54}$; highest: $\dfrac{11}{54}$

67. $10y - 8 - 2y = 4y - 22 + 5y$

Solve the equation. Which of the following is correct?

A) $y = -4\frac{2}{3}$

B) $y = 14$

C) $y = 30$

D) $y = -30$

68. Which of the following is equivalent to 37.5%?

A) 0.0375

B) 0.375

C) 3.75

D) 37.5

69. An employee makes $37,500 per year and receives a 5.5% raise. Which of the following is the employee's new salary?

A) $35,437.50

B) $35,625

C) $39,375

D) $39,562.50

70. Which of the following sets of numbers is listed in order from least to greatest?

A) $-0.95, 0, \frac{2}{5}, 0.35, \frac{3}{4}$

B) $-1, -\frac{1}{10}, -0.11, \frac{5}{6}, 0.75$

C) $-\frac{3}{4}, -0.2, 0, \frac{2}{3}, 0.55$

D) $-1.1, -\frac{4}{5}, -0.13, 0.7, \frac{9}{11}$

71. The population of a town was 7250 in 2014 and 7375 in 2015. Which of the following was the percent increase from 2014 to 2015? (Round to the nearest tenth.)

A) 1.5%

B) 1.6%

C) 1.7%

D) 1.8%

72. Which of the following choices places these fractions in the correct order from greatest to least?

$$\frac{1}{3}, -\frac{1}{4}, \frac{1}{2}, -\frac{1}{5}, \frac{1}{7}, -\frac{1}{6}$$

A) $\frac{1}{2}, \frac{1}{3}, \frac{1}{7}, -\frac{1}{5}, -\frac{1}{6}, -\frac{1}{4}$

B) $\frac{1}{2}, \frac{1}{3}, \frac{1}{7}, -\frac{1}{6}, -\frac{1}{5}, -\frac{1}{4}$

C) $\frac{1}{2}, \frac{1}{7}, \frac{1}{3}, -\frac{1}{4}, -\frac{1}{5}, -\frac{1}{6}$

D) $\frac{1}{2}, \frac{1}{3}, \frac{1}{7}, -\frac{1}{6}, -\frac{1}{4}, -\frac{1}{5}$

73. A sporting goods store is offering an additional 30% off all clearance items. Angie purchases a pair of running shoes on clearance for $65.00. If the shoes originally cost $85.00, what was her total discount?

A) 53.5%

B) 46.5%

C) 22.9%

D) 39.2%

74. Which of the following is not a rational number?

A) -4

B) $\frac{1}{5}$

C) $0.8\overline{33}$

D) $\sqrt{2}$

75. What is 1230.932567 rounded to the nearest hundredths place?

A) 1200

B) 1230.9326

C) 1230.93

D) 1230

76. What is the absolute value of -9?

A) -9

B) 9

C) 0

D) -1

77. Add $0.98 + 45.102 + 32.3333 + 31 + 0.00009$.

A) 368.573

B) 210.536299

C) 109.41539

D) 99.9975

78. $(9 \div 3) \times (8 \div 4) =$

A) 1

B) 6

C) 72

D) 576

79. $7.95 \div 1.5 =$

A) 2.4

B) 5.3

C) 6.2

D) 7.3

80. A bag contains twice as many red marbles as blue marbles, and the number of blue marbles is 88% of the number of green marbles. If g represents the number of green marbles, which of the following expressions represents the total number of marbles in the bag?

A) $3.88g$

B) $3.64g$

C) $2.64g$

D) $2.32g$

81. Melissa is ordering fencing to enclose a square area of 5625 square feet. How many feet of fencing does she need?

   A) 75

   B) 150

   C) 300

   D) 5,625

82. If a discount of 25% off the retail price of a desk saves Mark $45, what was the desk's original price?

   A) $135

   B) $160

   C) $180

   D) $210

83. Adam owns 4 times as many shirts as he has pairs of pants, and he has 5 pairs of pants for every 2 pairs of shoes. What is the ratio of Adam's shirts to Adam's shoes?

   A) 25 shirts: 1 pair shoes

   B) 10 shirts : 1 pair shoes

   C) 20 shirts : 1 pair shoes

   D) 15 shirts : 2 pairs shoes

84. Patrick is coming home from vacation in Costa Rica and wants to fill one of his suitcases with bags of Costa Rican coffee. The weight limit for his suitcase is 22 kilograms, and the suitcase itself weighs 3.2 kilograms. If each bag of coffee weighs 800 grams, how many bags can he bring in his suitcase without going over the limit?

   A) 2

   B) 4

   C) 23

   D) 27

85. Convert 0.28 into a fraction.

   A) $\frac{9}{25}$

   B) $\frac{7}{45}$

   C) $\frac{7}{25}$

   D) $\frac{8}{15}$

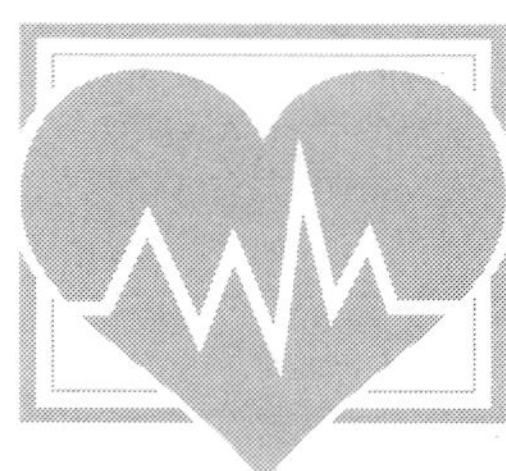

ANSWER KEY

1. C)

First calculate 20% of the list price:

$0.20 \times \$26{,}580 = \$5{,}316$

Next calculate the savings over the first 3 months of payments:

3 months $\times$ \$250/month $= \$750$

Find the total savings:

$\$5{,}316 + \$750 = \$6{,}066$

2. C)

First find the total cost before tax:

5 shirts $\times$ \$3/shirt $+$ 4 pants $\times$ \$6/pants $+$ 2 items mended $\times$ \$5/item mended $= \$49$

Now multiply this amount by 1.08 to account for the added 8% sales tax:

$\$49 \times 1.08 = \$52.92$

3. A)

Let s be the number of sandwiches sold. Each sandwich earns \$4, so selling s sandwiches at \$4 each results in revenue of \$4s. Similarly, d drinks at \$2 each gives \$2d of income and cookies bring in \$1c. Summing these values gives a total of revenue $= 4s + 2d + 1c$.

4. C)

The y-intercept will have an x value of 0. This eliminates choices A), B) and D). Plug $x = 0$ into the equation and solve for y to find the y-intercept:

$7y - 42(0) + 7 = 0$, so $7y = -7$ and therefore $y = -1$. The correct answer is $(0, -1)$, which is answer C).

5. C)

First complete the operations in parentheses:

$4 - \frac{1}{2^2} + 24 \div (8 + 12) = 4 - \frac{1}{2^2} + 24 \div (20)$

Next simplify the exponents:

$4 - \frac{1}{2^2} + 24 \div (20) = 4 - \frac{1}{4} + 24 \div (20)$

Then complete multiplication and division operations: $4 - \frac{1}{4} + 24 \div (20) = 4 - 0.25 + 1.2$

Finally complete addition and subtraction operations: $4 - 0.25 + 1.2 = 4.95$

6. A)

The area of a rectangle is *length* $\times$ *width*, so $A = L(3L)$. The area was given, so $1452 = 3L^2$

Solving for L: $484 = L^2$ and $L = \pm 22$.

Since length must be positive, $L = 22$ feet.

7. A)

Calculate the decline:

40% decline in 70% of the business $=$ $0.40 \times 0.70 = 0.28 = 28\%$ decline

Calculate the growth:

60% growth in 25% of the business $=$ $0.60 \times 0.25 = 0.15 = 15\%$ growth

Find the net change:

28% decline + 15% growth = $-0.28 + 0.15 =$
$-0.13 = 13\%$ decline

8.   D)

The first step is to multiply (resulting in 17.92); then divide the result by 0.4 (making 44.80 the solution).

9.   B)

First convert the dimensions to meters:

$15 \text{ ft.} \times \dfrac{1 \text{ m}}{3.28 \text{ ft.}} = 4.57 \text{ m}$

$9 \text{ ft.} \times \dfrac{1 \text{ m}}{3.28 \text{ ft.}} = 2.74 \text{ m}$

$12.5 \text{ ft.} \times \dfrac{1 \text{ m}}{3.28 \text{ ft.}} = 3.81 \text{ m}$

Next find the total area in square meters:

total area $= 2(4.57 \text{ m} \times 2.74 \text{ m}) + 2(3.81 \text{ m} \times 2.74 \text{ m}) = 45.9 \text{ m}^2$

Finally convert the area to gallons of paint:

$45.9 \text{ m}^2 \times \dfrac{1 \text{ gallon}}{32 \text{ m}^2} = 1.43 \text{ gallons}$

10.   D)

First convert mixed fractions to improper fractions:

$5\frac{2}{3} \times 1\frac{7}{8} \div \frac{1}{3} = \frac{17}{3} \times \frac{15}{8} \div \frac{1}{3}$

Next flip the divisor fraction and multiply:

$\frac{17}{3} \times \frac{15}{8} \div \frac{1}{3} = \frac{17}{3} \times \frac{15}{8} \times \frac{3}{1} =$

$\frac{17 \times 15 \times 3}{3 \times 8 \times 1} = \frac{765}{24}$

Now divide the numerator by the denominator to convert back to a mixed fraction:

$\frac{765}{24} = 31\frac{21}{24}$

Finally find the greatest common factor to reduce the fraction:

$31\frac{21}{24} = 31\frac{21 \div 3}{24 \div 3} = 31\frac{7}{8}$

11.   D)

A $\frac{3}{20}$ increase means the new wage is $w + w\left(\frac{3}{20}\right)$, or $w\left(1 + \frac{3}{20}\right)$.

Convert the fraction to decimal form:

$\frac{3}{20} = \frac{3}{20}\left(\frac{5}{5}\right) = \frac{15}{100} = 0.15$

The new wage is:

$w(1 + 0.15) = 1.15w$

12.   C)

In algebraic terms, the ratio can be expressed with the following equation:

$9x + 2x + 1x = 36$

Here, x represents some common factor by which each number of employees was divided to reduce the ratio. Solve for x, then find $2x$ to solve for the number of hosts:

$9x + 2x + 1x = 36$

$12x = 36$

$x = 3$

$2x = 2 \times 3 = 6$

13.   C)

$(1 - x) =$ proportion of men who do not play an instrument

$(1 - x) = \dfrac{\text{number of men who do not play an instrument}}{z}$

$(1 - x)z =$ number of men who do not play an instrument

14.   D)

Adding 20% is equivalent to paying 120% of the bill:

$\$48.30 \times \dfrac{120}{100} = \$57.96$

15.   C)

Convert the fractions to decimals:

$\frac{6}{9} \approx 0.67$

$\frac{1}{7} \approx 0.14$

Now order the numbers from smallest to largest:

$0.125 < 0.14 < 0.60 < 0.67$

16.   D)

Because the last decimal digit is in the hundredths place, the decimal part of the number is written as a fraction over 100. The fraction of $\frac{28}{100}$ reduces to $\frac{7}{25}$.

17.   B)

Start by multiplying both sides by 7:

$7(x \div 7) = 7(x - 36)$

$x = 7x - 252$

Now subtract $7x$ from both sides:

$x - 7x = 7x - 252 - 7x$

$-6x = -252$

Finally divide both sides by -6:

$\frac{-6x}{-6} = \frac{-252}{-6}$

$x = 42$

18. B)

A proportion is written using two ratios relating amount earned to months, with x representing the unknown amount:

$\frac{15,036}{7} = \frac{x}{2}$.

The proportion is solved by cross-multiplying and dividing: $7x = 30,072$, $x = 4,296$. The solution is \$4,296.

19. B)

The cost c of gas has units dollars per mile. Construct an expression that yields these units:

$$\frac{p}{m} = \frac{\left(\frac{\$}{\text{gal.}}\right)}{\left(\frac{\text{mi.}}{\text{gal.}}\right)} = \frac{(\$)(\text{gal.})}{(\text{mi.})(\text{gal.})} = \frac{\$}{\text{mi.}}$$

20. C)

Use the area to find the length of one side of the square:

$A = l \times w = l^2$

$5,625 \text{ ft.}^2 = l^2$

$l = \sqrt{5,625 \text{ ft.}^2} = 75 \text{ ft.}$

Now multiply the side length by 4 to find the perimeter:

$P = 4l$

$P = 4(75 \text{ ft.}) = 300 \text{ ft.}$

21. B)

Find the area of all of the sides of the shed. Two walls measure 5 feet by 7 feet; the other two walls measure 4 feet by 7 feet:

$A = 2l_1 w_1 + 2l_2 w_2$

$A = 2(5 \text{ ft.})(7 \text{ ft.}) + 2(4 \text{ ft.})(7 \text{ ft.})$

$A = 70 \text{ ft.}^2 + 56 \text{ ft.}^2 = 126 \text{ ft.}^2$

22. A)

The formula for the circumference of a circle is:

$C = 2\pi r$

Because $d = 2r$, this formula can be rewritten:

$C = \pi d$

$49 \text{ ft.} = \pi d$

$d = \frac{49 \text{ ft.}}{\pi} = 15.6 \text{ ft.}$

23. D)

To find the median, first order the data points from smallest to largest:

17, 25, 38, 41, 42, 45, 46, 50

There is an even number of data points. Locate the middle two points and take the average:

~~17, 25, 38,~~ 41, 42, ~~45, 46, 50~~

$(41 + 42) \div 2 = 41.5$

24. C)

Find Sam's income for each month:

January: \$900

February: \$1100

March: \$500

April: \$200

May: \$400

Now find the average by adding those values and dividing by 5. Then round to the nearest 100: $\frac{900 + 1100 + 500 + 200 + 400}{5} = 620 \approx 600$

25. B)

Since there are 16 ounces in a pound, 8 ounces = 0.5 pounds. The conversion factor of kilograms to pounds is therefore multiplied by 8.5 pounds. The calculation is:

$8.5 \text{ lb.} \left(\frac{1 \text{kg}}{2.2 \text{. lb.}}\right) = \frac{8.5}{2.2} = 3.9 \text{ kg.}$

Notice that the 1 is on top in this conversion factor so that pounds cancel. The unit that the quantity is being converted to must always be in the numerator.

26. D)

To add or subtract numbers in scientific notation, the exponents of the base of 10 must be the same. The first number can be rewritten as $4.71 \times 10 \times 10^2 = 47.1 \times 10^2$. The values in front of 10^2 are subtracted, and the power of 10 stays the same, with a result of 44.12×10^2. The solution is then rewritten in proper scientific notation as 4.412×10^3.

27. B)

The answer choices are −6, 0, −11, and −30 for A), B), C), and D), respectively. Answer choice B), 0, is the only response that is not negative.

28. D)

The algebraic expression can be simplified using PEMDAS.

$10^2 - 7(3 - 4) - 25 \rightarrow$

$10^2 - 7(-1) - 25 \rightarrow$

$100 + 7 - 25 \rightarrow$

$107 - 25 \rightarrow$

82

29. B)

The algebraic expression can be simplified using PEMDAS.

$$\frac{5^2(3) + 3(-2)^2}{4 + 3^2 - 2(5 - 8)} = \frac{5^2(3) + 3(-2)^2}{4 + 3^2 - 2(-3)} \rightarrow$$

$$\frac{25(3) + 3(4)}{4 + 9 - 2(-3)} = \frac{75 + 12}{13 + 6} = \frac{87}{19}$$

30. C)

First convert everything to kilograms:

$$800 \text{ g} \times \frac{1 \text{ kg}}{1,000 \text{ g}} = 0.8 \text{ kg}$$

$$300 \text{ g} \times \frac{1 \text{ kg}}{1,000 \text{ g}} = 0.3 \text{ kg}$$

Next find the total weight:

$1.2 \text{ kg} + 0.8 \text{ kg} + 0.3 \text{ kg} = 2.3 \text{ kg}$

Now find the total cost by multiplying by \$4/kg:

$$2.3 \text{ kg} \times \frac{\$4}{1 \text{ kg}} = \$9.20$$

31. B)

Each fraction is changed to an improper fraction: $\left(\frac{3}{2}\right)\left(\frac{8}{3}\right) \div \frac{5}{4}$.

Using PEMDAS and working left to right:

$$\left(\frac{3}{2}\right)\left(\frac{8}{3}\right) \div \frac{5}{4} = \frac{24}{6} \div \frac{5}{4} = \frac{4}{1} \div \frac{5}{4}.$$

To divide the fractions, the second fraction is flipped and then multiplied by the first fraction, giving $\left(\frac{4}{1}\right)\left(\frac{4}{5}\right) = \frac{16}{5}$.

This simplifies to $\frac{31}{5}$.

32. D)

First, simplify the exponents:

$$2^{-1} = \frac{1}{2^1} = \frac{1}{2}$$

$$(-1)^3 = -1$$

Now, order the quantities from most negative to most positive:

$$-\frac{4}{3}, -1, \frac{2}{5}, \frac{1}{2}$$

33. C)

The digit in the tenths place is 7 and is rounded up to 8 because the digit in the hundredths place is 8, which is greater than or equal to 5. So the number is rounded up to 2.8.

34. C)

A proportion is solved by cross-multiplying:

$$5(4x - 5) = \frac{3}{2}(2x - 6)$$

Then, the linear equation is solved for x:

$20x - 25 = 3x - 9; \ 17x = 16; \ x = \frac{16}{17}$.

35. D)

Start by adding 6 to both sides:

$8x - 6 + 6 = 3x + 24 + 6$

$8x = 3x + 30$

Next subtract $3x$ from both sides:

$8x - 3x = 3x + 30 - 3x$

$5x = 30$

Finally divide both sides by 5 to solve for x:

$5x \div 5 = 30 \div 5$

$x = 6$

36. D)

The solution can be written as a fraction by dividing the number of correct questions by the total number of questions: $\frac{42}{48} = 0.875$

Then, the result is multiplied by 100 for a grade of 87.5%.

37. D)

Substitute 5 for x:

$4(5) \div (5 - 1) = 20 \div 4 = 5$

38. C)

The slope of a horizontal line is zero because the change in y is zero.

39. C)

Alex and David split an appetizer that costs $8.50, so each will pay $4.25 in addition to the price of the entrée. Rachel orders an appetizer for $6.50, plus lemonade for $3, so she will pay $9.50 in addition to the price of the entrée.

$9.50 - $4.25 = $5.25

40. B)

Subtract the percentage of boys from 100% to find the percentage of girls:

$100\% - 46\% = 54\%$

Find 21% of 54% of 450:

$0.21 \times 0.54 \times 450 \approx 51$

41. C)

First convert 15,140 drops to seconds using the ratio given:

$15{,}140 \text{ drops} \times \frac{4 \text{ sec.}}{1 \text{ drop}} = 60{,}560 \text{ sec.}$

Now convert seconds to hours:

$60{,}560 \text{ sec.} \times \frac{1 \text{ min.}}{60 \text{ sec.}} \times \frac{1 \text{ hr.}}{60 \text{ min.}} = 16.8\overline{2} \text{ hr.}$

Convert the remainder of hours back to minutes and seconds:

$0.8\overline{2} \text{ hr.} \times \frac{60 \text{ min.}}{1 \text{ hr.}} = 49.\overline{3} \text{ min.}$

$0.\overline{3} \text{ min.} \times \frac{60 \text{ sec.}}{1 \text{ min.}} = 20 \text{ sec.}$

16 hours, 49 minutes, 20 seconds

42. D)

First complete the operations in parentheses:
$(3 + 5)^2 + 24 \div 16 - 5 \div 2 = (8)^2 + 24 \div 16 - 5 \div 2$

Next solve the exponents: $(8)^2 + 24 \div 16 - 5 \div 2$
$= 64 + 24 \div 16 - 5 \div 2$

Then complete multiplication and division operations: $64 + 24 \div 16 - 5 \div 2 = 64 + 1.5 - 2.5$

Finally complete addition and subtraction operations: $64 + 1.5 - 2.5 = 63$

43. C)

First convert the length of the race to miles:

$10 \text{ km} \times \frac{1{,}000 \text{ m}}{1 \text{ km}} \times \frac{1 \text{ ft.}}{0.3048 \text{ m}} \times \frac{1 \text{ mi.}}{5280 \text{ ft.}} = 6.21 \text{ mi.}$

Next convert her training pace to minutes (in decimal form):

$15 \text{ sec.} \times \frac{1 \text{ min.}}{60 \text{ sec.}} = 0.25 \text{ min.}$

$8 \text{ min.}, 15 \text{ sec.} = 8 \text{ min.} + 0.25 \text{ min.} = 8.25 \text{ min.}$

Then multiply the length of the race by her pace per mile:

$6.21 \text{ mi.} \times \frac{8.25 \text{ min.}}{1 \text{ mi.}} = 51.23 \text{ min.}$

Finally convert the time back to min:sec form:

$0.23 \text{ min.} \times \frac{60 \text{ sec.}}{1 \text{ min.}} = 14 \text{ sec.}$

51:14

44. D)

Flip the divisor fraction and multiply:

$\frac{8}{15} \div \frac{1}{6} = \frac{8}{15} \times \frac{6}{1} = \frac{8 \times 6}{15 \times 1} = \frac{48}{15}$

Then reduce the fraction by dividing numerator and denominator by the greatest common factor:

$\frac{48}{15} = \frac{48 \div 3}{15 \div 3} = \frac{16}{5}$

Finally divide the whole numbers to find the mixed fraction:

$\frac{16}{5} = 3\frac{1}{5}$

45. A)

$5\frac{1}{3}$ tbsp. of lemon juice should be used.

Set up a ratio:

$\frac{2 \text{ tbsp.}}{\frac{1}{4} \text{ c.}} = \frac{x}{\frac{2}{3} \text{ c.}}$

Now cross-multiply:

$(2 \text{ tbsp.})\left(\frac{2}{3} \text{ c.}\right) = (x)\left(\frac{1}{4} \text{ c.}\right)$

$x = \frac{\left(2 \text{ tbsp.}\left(\frac{2}{3} \text{ c.}\right)\right)}{\frac{1}{4} \text{ c.}} = 5\frac{1}{3} \text{ tbsp.}$

46. C)

$x = \frac{\text{female 9th graders}}{\text{total 9th grades}}$ and $y = \frac{\text{total 9th graders}}{\text{total students}}$

You are looking for the proportion $\frac{\text{female 9th graders}}{\text{total students}}$.

→

CONTINUE

See that multiplying x by y cancels out "total 9th graders" in the numerator and denominator and gives this proportion:

$$x \times y = \frac{\text{female 9th graders}}{\text{total 9th graders}} \times \frac{\text{total 9th graders}}{\text{total students}}$$

$$= \frac{\text{female 9th graders}}{\text{total students}}$$

47. A)

First calculate his original weekly work hours:

$$\frac{8 \text{ hr.}}{1 \text{ day}} \times \frac{5 \text{ days}}{1 \text{ wk.}} = \frac{40 \text{ hr.}}{\text{wk.}}$$

Next calculate his current weekly work hours:

$$\frac{8 \text{ hr}}{1 \text{ day}} \times \frac{3 \text{ days}}{1 \text{ wk.}} + \frac{4 \text{ hr.}}{1 \text{ day}} \times \frac{2 \text{ days}}{1 \text{ wk.}} = \frac{32 \text{ hr.}}{\text{wk.}}$$

Now find the difference in hours and divide by his original hours to find the percentage change:

$$\frac{\frac{40 \text{ hr.}}{\text{wk.}} - \frac{32 \text{ hr.}}{\text{wk.}}}{\frac{40 \text{ hr.}}{\text{wk.}}} = \frac{x}{100}$$

$$\left(\frac{8 \text{ hr.}}{\text{wk.}}\right)(100) = \left(\frac{40 \text{ hr.}}{\text{wk.}}\right)(x)$$

$$x = \frac{\left(\frac{8 \text{ hr.}}{\text{wk.}}\right)(100)}{\left(\frac{40 \text{ hr.}}{\text{wk.}}\right)} = 20$$

Toledo's weekly work hours have decreased by 20%.

48. A)

Convert fractions to a common denominator and compare numerators:

$$\frac{2}{16} = \frac{6}{48}$$

$$\frac{1}{24} = \frac{2}{48}$$

$$\frac{3}{32} = \frac{4.5}{48}$$

$$\frac{3}{16} = \frac{9}{48}$$

$$\frac{2}{48} < \frac{4.5}{48} < \frac{5}{48} < \frac{6}{48} < \frac{9}{48}$$

49. A)

First subtract 4 from both sides:

$$3a + 4 - 4 = 2a - 4$$

$$3a = 2a - 4$$

Next subtract $2a$ from both sides (remember that the minus sign remains before the 4):

$$3a - 2a = 2a - 4 - 2a$$

$$a = -4$$

50. D)

A proportion is written using two ratios relating pages to minutes, with x representing the number of unknown minutes: $\frac{40}{45} = \frac{265}{x}$. The proportion is solved by cross-multiplying and dividing: $40x = 11,925$, $x = 298.125$. The solution is approximately 298 minutes.

51. D)

The money Jane earns is equal to $15 times the number of hours she babysits:

$15h$

The total money in Jane's bank account is equal to the money she started with plus the money she earns:

$275 + 15h$

Set this expression equal to $400:

$400 = 275 + 15h$

52. C)

This rectangular prism has 2 sides that are 12 inches by 18 inches, 2 sides that are 12 inches by 6 inches, and 2 sides that are 18 inches by 6 inches. Add the area of all the sides to find the total surface area:

$$SA = 2lw + 2lh + 2wh$$

$$SA = 2(12 \text{ in.})(18 \text{ in.}) + 2(12 \text{ in.})(6 \text{ in.}) + 2(18 \text{ in.})(6 \text{ in.})$$

$$SA = 432 \text{ in.}^2 + 144 \text{ in.}^2 + 216 \text{ in.}^2 = 792 \text{ in.}^2$$

53. C)

The answer choices are 24, -2, 30, and 0 for A, B, C, and D, respectively. Answer choice C, 30, is the greatest value for all of the responses.

54. B)

First find the radius of the pizza:

$$r = \frac{d}{2}$$

$$r = \frac{10 \text{ in.}}{2} = 5 \text{ in.}$$

Next use the formula for sector area:

$$A = \pi r^2 \frac{\theta}{360°}$$

$$A = \pi(5 \text{ in.})^2 \left(\frac{40°}{360°}\right) = 8.7 \text{ in.}^2$$

55. A)

The mean is equal to the sum of the results divided by the number of results:

$$\frac{1+3+5+x}{4} = 2.5$$

$$1 + 3 + 5 + x = 10$$

$$x = 1$$

56. C)

To find the mean, divide the sum of the data points by the number of data points:

Mean of seventh graders $= \frac{2+1+1+2+2}{5} = 1.6$

Mean of tenth graders $= \frac{0+1+1+0}{4} = 0.5$

Now find the difference:

$$1.6 - 0.5 = 1.1$$

57. D)

The conversion factor of meters to feet is multiplied by 55 meters. The calculation is

$$55\,\text{m}\left(\frac{3.28\ \text{ft.}}{1\ \text{m}}\right) = 180.4\ \text{feet}$$

58. C)

The algebraic expression can be simplified using PEMDAS:

$$-(3)^2 + (5-7)^2 - 3(4-8)$$

$$= -(3)^2 + (-2)^2 - 3(-4)$$

$$= -9 + 4 - 3(-4)$$

$$= -9 + 4 + 12$$

$$= 7$$

59. B)

Divide the percentage who enrolled at a small public university by the total percentage who enrolled in a public university:

$$\frac{11\%}{11\% + 38\%} = 22\%$$

60. D)

The algebraic expression can be simplified using PEMDAS:

$$(3^2 \div 1^3) - (4 - 8^2) + 2^4$$

$$= (9 \div 1) - (4 - 64) + 16$$

$$= 9 - (-60) + 16$$

$$= 85.$$

61. B)

The first step is to subtract (resulting in -1.88); then add the result to 14.2 (making 12.32 the solution). Line up decimal points when adding or subtracting.

62. A)

First, find the radius:

$$r = \frac{d}{2}$$

$$r = \frac{5\ \text{in.}}{2} = 2.5\ \text{in.}$$

Now use the formula for the volume of a cylinder:

$$V = \pi r^2 h$$

$$V = \pi(2.5\ \text{in.})^2(9\ \text{in.}) = 176.6\ \text{in.}^2$$

63. B)

The least common denominator (LCD) for the three fractions is 120. To find the LCD, write each of the denominators in prime factorization form: $8 = 2^3$, $10 = 2 \times 5$, $3 = 3 \times 1$. The least common multiple of 8, 10, and 3 is the product of all the prime numbers in these factorizations to their highest power. So the LCD $= 2^3 \times 3 \times 5 = 120$.

To write each fraction in equivalent form with a denominator of 120, the first fraction is multiplied by $\frac{15}{15}$, the second fraction is multiplied by $\frac{12}{12}$, and the third fraction is multiplied by $\frac{40}{40}$. The problem is now:

$$\frac{105}{120} - \frac{12}{120} - \frac{80}{120} = \frac{93}{120} - \frac{80}{120} = \frac{13}{120}$$

64. D)

The fraction $\frac{10}{11}$ is changed to a decimal by long dividing 11 into 10 with the result of 0.909090... Therefore, the solution is $4.\overline{90}$ since the decimal repeats.

65. A)

The digit in the hundreds place is 3. It is rounded up to 4 because the digit in the tens place is 6, which is greater than or equal to 5. The number is thus rounded up to 74,400. The digit in the thousands place is 4, and remains 4 because the digit in the hundreds place (3) is less than 5. The number is therefore rounded to 74,000.

66. C)

The total amount of sales for the week is \$2,700. The lowest amount of sales was on Tuesday and the largest was on Saturday. The ratio for Tuesday is $\frac{250}{2700} = \frac{5}{54}$ and the ratio for Saturday is $\frac{800}{2700} = \frac{8}{27}$.

67. B)

Start by combining like terms on each side:

$8y - 8 = 9y - 22$

Next, subtract $8y$ from both sides:

$8y - 8 - 8y = 9y - 22 - 8y$

$-8 = y - 22$

Finally, add 22 to both sides:

$-8 + 22 = y - 22 + 22$

$y = 14$

68. B)

Changing a percent to a decimal requires that the decimal point be moved two places to the left. Moving the decimal in 37.5 to the left two places results in 0.375.

69. D)

The first step is to find the amount of change by multiplying 37,500 by 0.055 (5.5% written as a decimal), which is \$2,062.50. The amount of change, added to the original salary, is \$39,562.50.

Alternatively, recognize the fact that the employee is now earning 105.5% of what he or she earned before. Calculate the new salary by multiplying $1.055 \times 37,500 = 39,562.50$.

70. D)

The values are easily compared if all are written in decimal form. The decimal values for D are $-1.1, -0.8, -0.13, 0.7$, and $.\overline{81}$. This is the only answer choice listed from least to greatest.

71. C)

The percent of change is the amount of change divided by the original amount, multiplied by 100. The amount of change is $7375 - 7250 = 125$. The percent change is $\frac{125}{7250} \times 100 = 1.7\%$.

72. B)

Since all the numerators are the same, the numbers can be ordered by comparing the denominators. The largest positive fractions have the smallest denominators (since dividing by larger numbers creates smaller fractions). For the negative fractions, the fraction closest to 0 (and therefore the largest) will be the one with the smallest absolute value (and largest denominator). Alternately, each of the fractions can be changed to decimals as $0.\overline{3}, -0.25, 0.5, -0.2, 0.\overline{42857}, -0.1\overline{6}$. The fractions written in order from greatest to least are $\frac{1}{2}, \frac{1}{3}, \frac{1}{7}, -\frac{1}{6}, -\frac{1}{5}, -\frac{1}{4}$.

73. B)

First, take the additional 30% off the clearance price:

$\$65.00 \times \frac{70}{100} = \$45.50$

Next, find what percentage of \$85.00 is \$45.50:

$\frac{\$45.50}{\$85.00} = \frac{x}{100}$

$(\$45.50)(100) = (\$85.00)(x)$

$x = \frac{(\$45.50)(100)}{\$85.00} = 53.5$

Angie is paying 53.5% the original price, which means she received a $100\% - 53.5\% = 46.5\%$ discount.

74. D)

A rational number is one which can be written in the form of a simple fraction. If we observe closely, only option D) gives us a number which cannot be written in the form of a fraction.

75. C)

We are asked to round off this given number to the nearest hundredths place. Considering the numbers on the right of the decimal, our answer comes out to be 1230.93.

76. B)

We know that the absolute value of any negative number gives the positive of that same number (i.e. absolute value of -9 is $+9$).

77. C)

There are two ways to solve this question. First, you can add all the given numbers and find the exact answer. This method is time-consuming and is less efficient.

The second method to solve this question is by adding only the numbers on the left of the decimal and then comparing your answer with the answer choices that you are given. We add

45, 32, and 31 to get $45 + 32 + 31 = 108$. Now, we can easily interpret that our answer must be very close to 108 when we add the decimal points as well for each given number. In the answer choices, only option C) gives us the number closest to 108. (Note that this method of approximation saves time but it is not very accurate if all the answer choices are very close to each other.)

78.   B)

This is a very simple question. All you need to know is the PEMDAS rule. First of all, solve the problems inside the parentheses, and then we multiply the answers of each.

9 divided by 3 equals 3.

8 divided by 4 equals 2.

We multiply 3 and 2 to get our final answer: $3 \times 2 = 6$

79.   B)

This is a simple division question. When we divide 7.95 by 1.5, we get 5.3 as answer. In order to re-confirm your answer, you can cross-check by multiplying 5.3 by 1.5, and it would be 7.95.

80.   B)

There are twice as many red marbles as blue marbles, so (red) = 2(blue).

The number of blue marbles is 88% the number of green marbles, so (blue) = $0.88g$.

Substitute this expression for blue marbles in the one above:

(red) = $2(0.88g)$

(red) = $1.76g$

The total number of marbles is equal to red plus blue plus green:

(red) + (blue) + g

$1.76g + 0.88g + g$

$3.64g$

81.   C)

Use the area to find the length of a side of the square:

$A = l \times w = l^2$

$5{,}625 \text{ ft}^2 = l^2$

$l = \sqrt{5{,}625 \text{ ft}^2} = 75 \text{ ft}$

Now multiply the side length by 4 to find the perimeter:

$P = 4l$

$P = 4(75 \text{ ft}) = 300 \text{ ft}$

82.   C)

From the given information in the question, we know that 25% of the actual price of a desk is $45. If we write this in the form of an equation, it becomes:

$\left(\frac{25}{100}\right) \times x = \$45$ (25% of x equals \$45)

$x = \frac{45}{0.25} \rightarrow \$180$

Therefore, the actual price of the desk equals $180.

83.   B)

Multiply the ratios so that pants cancel out in the numerator and denominator:

$$\frac{4 \text{ shirts}}{1 \text{ pants}} \times \frac{5 \text{ pants}}{2 \text{ pairs shoes}} = \frac{20 \text{ shirts}}{2 \text{ pairs shoes}}$$

Divide by the greatest common factor to reduce the ratio:

$$\frac{20 \text{ shirts}}{2 \text{ pairs shoes}} \div 2 = \frac{10 \text{ shirts}}{1 \text{ pair shoes}}$$

84.   C)

$22 \text{ kg} - 3.2 \text{ kg} = 18.8 \text{ kg}$ remaining for coffee

$18.8 \text{ kg} = 18{,}800 \text{ g}$

$$18{,}800 \text{ g} \times \frac{1 \text{ bag of coffee}}{800 \text{ g}} = 23.5 \text{ bags of coffee}$$

Round down to 23 bags.

85.   C)

$0.28 = \frac{28}{100}$

The lowest common denominator is 4.

$\frac{28}{4} = 7$

$\frac{100}{4} = 25$

$= \frac{7}{25}$

READING

Directions: Read the question, passage, or figure carefully, and choose the best answer.

1. The social and political discourse of America continues to be permeated with idealism. An idealistic viewpoint asserts that the ideals of freedom, equality, justice, and human dignity are the truths that Americans must continue to aspire to. Idealists argue that truth is what should be, not necessarily what is. In general, they work to improve things and to make them as close to ideal as possible.

   Which of the following best captures the author's purpose?

   A) to advocate for freedom, equality, justice, and human rights

   B) to explain what an idealist believes in

   C) to explain what's wrong with social and political discourse in America

   D) to persuade readers to believe in certain truths

2. The diagram represents a blood pressure monitor. Which of the following represents the systolic blood pressure reading?

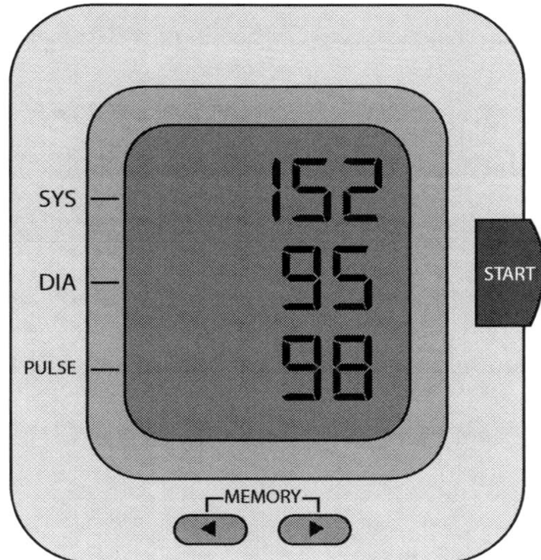

   A) 152

   B) 95

   C) 98

   D) $\frac{152}{95}$

The next four questions are based on this passage.

The best friend a man has in the world may turn against him and become his enemy. His son or daughter that he has reared with loving care may prove ungrateful. Those who are nearest and dearest to us, those whom we trust with our happiness and our good name may become traitors to their faith. The money that a man has, he may lose. It flies away from him, perhaps when he needs it most. A man's reputation may be sacrificed in a moment of ill-considered action.

The one absolutely unselfish friend that man can have in this selfish world, the one that never deserts him, the one that never proves ungrateful or treacherous is his dog. A man's dog stands by him in prosperity and in poverty, in health and in sickness. He will sleep on the cold ground, where the wintry winds blow and the snow drives fiercely, if only he may be near his master's side. He will kiss the hand that has no food to offer. He will lick the wounds and sores that come in encounters with the roughness of the world. He guards the sleep of his pauper master as if he were a prince. When all other friends desert, he remains.

George Graham Vest - c. 1855
http://www.historyplace.com/speeches/vest.htm

3. Which of the following best describes the structure of the text?

    A) chronology

    B) cause and effect

    C) problem and solution

    D) contrast

4. Which of the following could be considered the topic of this passage?

    A) loyal friends

    B) misfortune

    C) human treachery

    D) feeling safe

5. Which of the following is a logical conclusion of the passage?

    A) Those closest to you will always betray you.

    B) Friendships with other people are pointless.

    C) Someone who wants a loyal friend should get a dog.

    D) Only a dog can help a person through the rough times in his or her life.

6. Which of the following is the purpose of this passage?

    A) to inform

    B) to entertain

    C) to describe

    D) to persuade

The next two questions are based on this passage.

How to Plant Potatoes

Before Planting

Plant potatoes no later than 2 weeks after the last spring freeze.

Cut potatoes into pieces 1 to 2 days before planting.

Loosen soil using a tiller or hand trowel.

Mix fertilizer or compost into loosened soil.

Planting

Dig a 4-inch-deep trench and place potatoes 1 foot apart.

Cover potatoes loosely with soil.

After Planting

Water immediately after planting, and then regularly afterward to keep soil moist.

After 6 weeks, mound soil around the base of the plant to ensure roots stay covered.

7. Which of the following is the first step to take after planting potatoes?

   A) Mound soil around the base of the plant.

   B) Water immediately.

   C) Mix fertilizer or compost into loosened soil.

   D) Place potatoes 1 foot apart.

8. Which of the following should be done after the soil has been loosened with a tiller or trowel?

   A) Mix fertilizer or compost into loosened soil.

   B) Dig a 4-inch-deep trench.

   C) Cut potatoes into pieces.

   D) Mound soil around the base of the plant.

The next two questions are based on this email.

Alan —

   I just wanted to drop you a quick note to let you know I'll be out of the office for the next two weeks. Elizabeth and I are finally taking that trip to France we've been talking about for years. It's a bit of a last-minute decision, but since we had the vacation time available, we figured it was now or never.

   Anyway, my team's been briefed on the upcoming meeting, so they should be able to handle the presentation without any hiccups. If you have any questions or concerns, you can direct them to Joanie, who'll be handling my responsibilities while I'm out.

   Let me know if you want any special treats. I don't know if you can take chocolate and cheese on the plane, but I'm going to try!

   Best regards,

   Michael

9. Which of the following most likely describes the relationship between the author and Alan?

   A) familial

   B) formal

   C) friendly

   D) strained

10. Which of the following best captures the author's purpose?

   A) to ask Alan if he wants any special treats from France

   B) to brag to Alan about his upcoming vacation

   C) to inform Alan that he will be out of the office

   D) to help Alan prepare for the upcoming meeting

CONTINUE

The next two questions are based on this map.

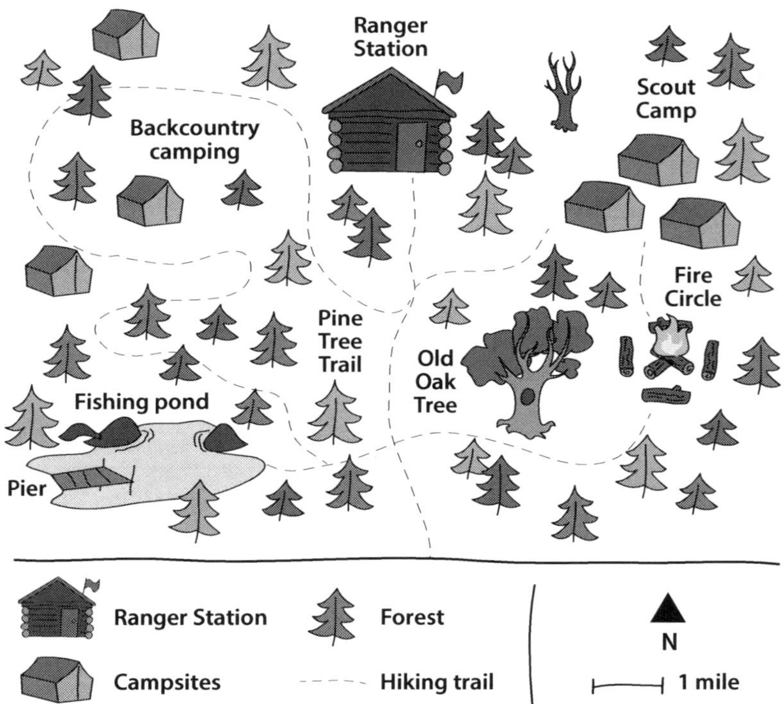

11. Which of the following is located due north of the Fire Circle?

   A) Old Oak Tree

   B) Scout Camp

   C) Fishing Pond

   D) Backcountry Camping

12. If a camper followed the trail from the Fishing Pond to the Scout Camp and passed by the Fire Circle, which of the following would she also have to pass by?

   A) Old Oak Tree

   B) Ranger Station

   C) Backcountry Camping

   D) Pier

The next three questions are based on this passage.

Carl's Car Depot is hosting its one-day-only summer sale event! All sedans, trucks, SUVs, and more are marked to move quickly. We're offering no money down and low (like, really low) monthly payments. You won't find prices like these anywhere else in the city (or the state, or anywhere else you look). No matter what you're looking for, we've the new and used cars you need. We only drop our prices this low once a year, so don't miss out on this great deal!

13. Which of the following best describes the author's purpose?

   A) The author wants to tell customers what kinds of cars are available at Carl's Car Depot.

   B) The author wants to encourage other car dealerships to lower their prices.

   C) The author wants to provide new and used cars at affordable prices.

   D) The author wants to attract customers to Carl's Car Depot.

14. Based on the context, which of the following is the meaning of the word *move* in the passage?

   A) drive

   B) sell

   C) advance forward

   D) change location

15. Which of the following is NOT mentioned by the author as a reason to visit Carl's Car Depot?

   A) They are offering lifetime warranties on new cars.

   B) The sale will only last one day.

   C) They have the lowest prices in town.

   D) They are offering no money down and low monthly payments.

16. Although Ben *said* he supported for his coworkers, his actions suggested he did not condone their behavior.

Italics are used for which of the following reasons?

   A) to show a word is intentionally misspelled

   B) to indicate a word in a foreign language

   C) to emphasize a contrast

   D) to reference a footnote

The next five questions are based on this passage.

It had been a long morning for Julia. She'd been woken up early by the sound of lawn mowers outside her window, and despite her best efforts, had been unable to get back to sleep. So, she'd reluctantly got out of bed, showered, and prepared her morning cup of coffee. At least, she tried to anyway. In the kitchen she'd discovered she was out of regular coffee and had to settle for a decaffeinated cup instead.

Once on the road, her caffeine-free mug of coffee didn't help make traffic less annoying. In fact, it seemed to Julia like the other drivers were sluggish and surly as well—it took her an extra fifteen minutes to get to work. And when she arrived, all the parking spots were full.

By the time she'd finally found a spot in the overflow lot, she was thirty minutes late for work. She'd hoped her boss would be too busy to notice, but he'd already put a pile of paperwork on her desk with a note that simply said "Rewrite." She wondered if she should point out to her boss that she hadn't been the one to write the reports in the first place, but decided against it.

When the fire alarm went off an hour later, Julia decided she'd had enough. She grabbed her purse and headed outside with her coworkers. While everyone else stood around waiting for the alarm to quiet, Julia determinedly walked to her car, fired up the engine, and set a course for home.

17. Which of the following lists Julia's actions in the correct sequence?

   A) Julia woke up early and found she didn't have any regular coffee. When she got to work, her boss had a lot for her to do. When the fire alarm went off, she decided to go home.

   B) Julia got to work and decided she was too tired to do the work her boss asked for, so she went home to get a cup of coffee.

   C) Julia woke up when the fire alarm went off and couldn't get back to sleep. She then got stuck in traffic and arrived at work thirty minutes late.

   D) Julia was woken up early by a lawnmower and then got stuck in traffic on the way to her office. Once there, she found that the office was out of coffee and she had a lot of work to do. When the fire alarm went off, she decided to go home.

18. Which of the following is the most likely reason Julia did not return to work after the alarm?

   A) She was embarrassed that should could not finish the work her boss asked for.

   B) She was tired and wanted to go home.

   C) She got stuck in traffic and could not get back to her office.

   D) Her boss gave her the afternoon off.

19. Which of the following statements based on the passage should be considered an opinion?

   A) Julia's boss asked her to do work to help one of her coworkers.

   B) Julia was late to work because of traffic.

   C) It was irresponsible for Julia to leave work early.

   D) Julia was tired because she'd been woken up early.

20. The passage states that Julia *set a course for home*. Which of the following is the most accurate interpretation of this sentence?

A) Julia is looking up directions to her house.

B) Julia is planning to drive home.

C) Julia wants to go home but will go back to work.

D) Julia is worried the fire at her office will spread to her home.

21. Which of the following conclusions is best supported by the passage?

A) Julia will find a job closer to her home.

B) Julia will be fired.

C) Julia will feel guilty and return to work.

D) Julia will drive home and go to sleep.

22. Alexander Hamilton and James Madison called for the Constitutional Convention to write a constitution as the foundation of a stronger federal government. Madison and other Federalists like John Adams believed in separation of powers, republicanism, and a strong federal government. Despite the separation of powers that would be provided for in the US Constitution, anti-Federalists like Thomas Jefferson called for even more limitations on the power of the federal government.

In the context of the passage above, which of the following would most likely NOT support a strong federal government?

A) Alexander Hamilton

B) James Madison

C) John Adams

D) Thomas Jefferson

23. Based on the pattern in the headings, which of the following is a reasonable heading to insert in the blank spot?

Chapter 2: Amphibians of Texas

1.   Frogs
        A) Tree Frogs
        B) __________
        C) True Frogs
2.   Toads
        A) True Toads
        B) Narrowmouth Toads
        C) Burrowing Toads
3.   Salamanders

A) Gray Tree Frog

B) Tropical Frogs

C) Newts

D) Spadefoot Toads

24. Which of the following is an example of a secondary source that would be used in a documentary about World War I?

A) an essay by a historian about the lasting effects of the war

B) photographs of military equipment used in the war

C) a recorded interview with a veteran who fought for the US Army

D) letters written by soldiers to their families

25. Victoria won easily and had plenty of time to rest before her next scheduled match.

Based on the context, which of the following is the meaning of the word *match* in the sentence?

A) a competitive event

B) a suitable pair

C) a slender piece of wood used to start a fire

D) a prospective marriage partner

The next two questions are based on this table.

Table 1.1. Book Sales by Distributor

DISTRIBUTOR	COST STRUCTURE
Wholesale Books	$100 for the first 25 books; $80 for every 25 additional books
The Book Barn	$98 for every 25 books
Books and More	$3.99 per book
Quarter Price Books	$3.99 per book for the first 25 books; $2.99 for each additional book

26. A school wants to buy seventy-five textbooks. Based on the pricing chart, which of the following distributors would offer the cheapest price for the books?

A) Wholesale Books

B) The Book Barn

C) Books and More

D) Quarter Price Books

27. A teacher wants to buy an additional twenty-five books for her classroom. If she orders her books separately, which distributor would offer the cheapest price?

A) Wholesale Books

B) The Book Barn

C) Books and More

D) Quarter Price Books

The next two questions are based on this passage.

The study showed that private tutoring is providing a significant advantage to those students who are able to afford it. Researchers looked at the grades of students who had received free tutoring through the school versus those whose parents had paid for private tutors. The study included 2500 students in three high schools across four grade levels. The study found that private tutoring corresponded with a rise in grade point average (GPA) of 0.5 compared to students who used the school's free tutor service and 0.7 compared to students who used no tutoring. After reviewing the study, the board is recommending that the school restructure its free tutor service to provide a more equitable education for all students.

28. Which of the following would weaken the author's argument?

A) the fact that the cited study was funded by a company that provides discounted tutoring through schools

B) a study showing differences in standardized test scores between students at schools in different neighborhoods

C) a statement signed by local teachers stating that they do not provide preferential treatment in the classroom or when grading

D) a study showing that GPA does not strongly correlate with success in college

29. Which of the following types of arguments is used in the passage?

A) emotional argument

B) appeal to authority

C) specific evidence

D) rhetorical questioning

CONTINUE

30. Start with the shapes shown below. Follow the directions.

A B C D E F

1. Remove block C.
2. Remove block E.
3. Place block A immediately after block D.
4. Add block C after block A.

Which of the following shows the order in which the shapes now appear?

A) B D A F

B) B D A E F

C) B D A C F

D) B D F A C

The next two questions are based on this passage.

After looking at five houses, Robert and I have decided to buy the one on Forest Road. The first two homes we visited didn't have the space we need—the first had only one bathroom, and the second did not have a guest bedroom. The third house, on Pine Street, had enough space inside but didn't have a big enough yard for our three dogs. The fourth house we looked at, on Rice Avenue, was stunning but well above our price range. The last home, on Forest Road, wasn't in the neighborhood we wanted to live in. However, it had the right amount of space for the right price.

31. Which of the following lists the author's actions in the correct sequence?

A) The author looked at the house on Forest Road, then at a house with a yard that was too small, then at two houses that were too small, and then finally at a house that was too expensive.

B) The author looked at the house on Forest Road, then at two houses that were too small, then at a house with a yard that was too small, and then finally at a house that was too expensive.

C) The author looked at two homes with yards that were too small, then a house with only one bathroom, then a house that was too expensive, and then finally the house on Forest Road.

D) The author looked at two homes that were too small, then a house with a yard that was too small, then a house that was too expensive, and then finally at the house on Forest Road.

32. What is the author's conclusion about the house on Pine Street?

A) The house did not have enough bedrooms.

B) The house did not have a big enough yard.

C) The house was not in the right neighborhood.

D) The house was too expensive.

33. A student wants to find unbiased information on an upcoming state senate election for a class project. Which of the following sources should the student use?

A) a website run by a candidate's campaign advisor

B) an endorsement of a candidate from a local newspaper

C) a blog run by a local radio personality

D) a book on the history of elections

The next two questions are based on this passage.

Mr. Tim Morgan —

This letter is to inform Mr. Morgan that his application for the position of Lead Technician has been received by our Human Resources team. We have been pleased to receive a higher-than-expected number of applications for this position, and we are glad that Mr. Morgan is among the many who find our company an attractive place to build a career. Due to the influx of applications, our Human Resources team will be taking longer than previously stated to review candidates and schedule interviews. Please look for further communication from our Human Resources team in the next two to three weeks.

Regards,

Allison Wakefield

Head of Human Resources

34. Which of the following best describes the purpose of the passage?

A) to let Mr. Morgan know that he will likely not receive an offer for the job of Lead Technician due to the high number of applicants

B) to express to Mr. Morgan how pleased the Human Resources team was to receive his application

C) to offer Mr. Morgan the position of Lead Technician

D) to inform Mr. Morgan that the review of candidates will take longer than expected

35. Which of the following conclusions is well supported by the passage?

A) The Human Resources team had previously informed Mr. Morgan that he would receive feedback on his application in less than two weeks.

B) Mr. Morgan is well qualified for the position of Lead Technician and will be offered an interview.

C) The Human Resources team will have trouble finding a qualified candidate for the position of Lead Technician.

D) Mr. Morgan will respond to this communication by removing himself from consideration for the positon of Lead Technician.

The next three questions are based on this passage.

The greatest changes in sensory, motor, and perceptual development happen in the first two years of life. When babies are first born, most of their senses operate in a similar way to those of adults. For example, babies are able to hear before they are born; studies show that babies turn toward the sound of their mothers' voices just minutes after being born, indicating they recognize the mother's voice from their time in the womb.

The exception to this rule is vision. A baby's vision changes significantly in its first year of life; initially it has a range of vision of only 8 – 12 inches and no depth perception. As a result, infants rely primarily on hearing; vision does not become the dominant sense until around the age of 12 months. Babies also prefer faces to other objects. This preference, along with their limited vision range, means that their sight is initially focused on their caregiver.

36. Which of the following is a concise summary of the passage?

A) Babies have no depth perception until 12 months, which is why they focus only on their caregivers' faces.

B) Babies can recognize their mothers' voices when born, so they initially rely primarily on their sense of hearing.

C) Babies have senses similar to those of adults except for their sense of sight, which doesn't fully develop until 12 months.

D) Babies' senses go through many changes in the first year of their lives.

37. Which of the following senses do babies primarily rely on?

A) vision

B) hearing

C) touch

D) smell

38. Which of the following best describes the mode of the passage?

A) expository

B) narrative

C) persuasive

D) descriptive

39. According to the guide, in which of the following seasons would ginger be harvested?

> **Spring**: artichokes, broccoli, chives, collard greens, peas, spinach, watercress
>
> **Summer**: beets, bell peppers, corn, eggplant, green beans, okra, tomatoes, zucchini
>
> **Fall**: acorn squash, brussels sprouts, cauliflower, endive, ginger, sweet potatoes
>
> **Winter**: Belgian endive, buttercup squash, kale, leeks, turnips, winter squash

A) spring

B) summer

C) fall

D) winter

40. Based on the pattern in the headings, which of the following is a reasonable heading to insert in the blank spot?

> 3.   Balanced Nutrition
>
>   A. Sources of iron
>
>   1) Animal-based sources
>
>   a. Beef
>
>   b. Pork
>
>   c. __________
>
>   2) Plant-based sources
>
>   a. Leafy greens
>
>   b. Nuts and seeds
>
>   B. Sources of calcium

A) Dairy

B) Lamb

C) Legumes

D) Vitamins

The next two questions are based on this passage.

In Greek mythology, two gods, Epimetheus and Prometheus, were given the work of creating living things. Epimetheus gave good powers to the different animals. To the lion he gave strength; to the bird, swiftness; to the fox, sagacity; and so on. Eventually, all of the good gifts had been bestowed, and there was nothing left for humans. As a result, Prometheus returned to heaven and brought down fire, which he gave to humans. With fire, human beings could protect themselves by making weapons. Over time, humans developed civilization.

41. Which of the following provides the best summary of the passage?

A) Epimetheus was asked to assign all the good traits to the animals, which upset Prometheus. In retaliation, Prometheus brought fire to humans, which allowed them to reign over the other animals.

B) Epimetheus and Prometheus were both asked to create living things and assign traits to living creatures. Epimetheus gave all of the positive traits to the other animals and left nothing for humans, so Prometheus brought humans fire. This fire allowed human beings to thrive.

C) Epimetheus and Prometheus were given the job of assigning traits to the animals. They decided to give strength to lions, swiftness to birds, sagacity to the fox, and fire to humans. This fire has helped humans grow to be superior to other animals.

D) Prometheus decided that humans needed fire to protect themselves from the other animals. He brought fire down from Heaven and taught humans how to make weapons, which allowed humans to hunt animals.

42. Which of the following is the meaning of the word *bestowed* as it is used in the passage?

A) purchased

B) forgotten

C) accepted

D) given

The next two questions are based on this excerpt.

Table of Contents

43. A student wants to find information on the Italian painter Sandro Botticelli. On which of the following pages will the student most likely find this information?

A) 55

B) 71

C) 95

D) 114

44. A student wants to find information on a church built in 1518. On which of the following pages should the student begin to look for this information?

A) 59

B) 105

C) 153

D) 179

The next two questions are based on this passage.

As you can see from the graph, my babysitting business has been really successful. The year started with a busy couple of months—several snows combined with a large number of requests for Valentine's Day services boosted our sales quite a bit. The spring months have admittedly been a bit slow, but we're hoping for a big summer once school gets out. Several clients have already put in requests for our services!

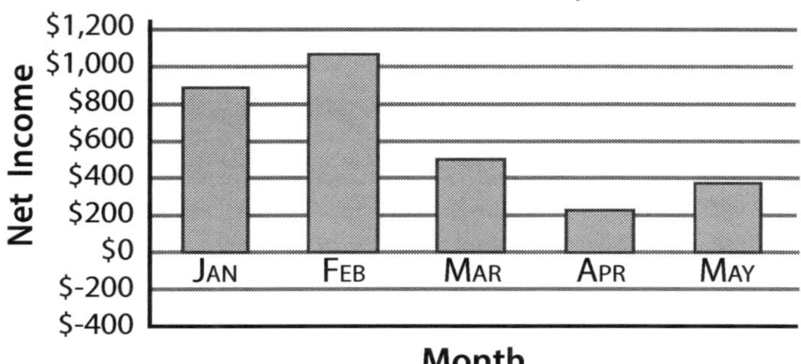

45. Based on the information in the graph, how much more did Sam's Babysitting Service bring in during February than during April?

A) $200

B) $900

C) $1100

D) $1300

46. Which of the following best describes the tone of the passage?

A) professional

B) casual

C) concerned

D) neutral

The odds of success for any new restaurant are slim. Competition in the city is fierce, and the low margin of return means that aspiring restaurateurs must be exact and ruthless with their budget and pricing. The fact that The Hot Dog has lasted as long as it has is a testament to its owners' skills.

47. Which of the following conclusions is well supported by the passage?

A) The Hot Dog offers the best casual dining in town.

B) The Hot Dog has a well-managed budget and prices items on its menu appropriately.

C) The popularity of The Hot Dog will likely fall as new restaurants open in the city.

D) The Hot Dog has a larger margin of return than other restaurants in the city.

48. Which of the following is the meaning of *testament* as used in the sentence?

A) story

B) surprise

C) artifact

D) evidence

49. Which of the following sentences indicates the end of a sequence?

A) Our ultimate objective was to find a quality coat at an affordable price.

B) We chose this particular restaurant because of its outdoor seating.

C) Finally, we were able to settle in to enjoy the movie.

D) Initially, it seemed unlikely that we'd be able to keep the puppy.

50. The diagram represents the lock and key model of enzymes. According to the figure, the products are formed from which of the following?

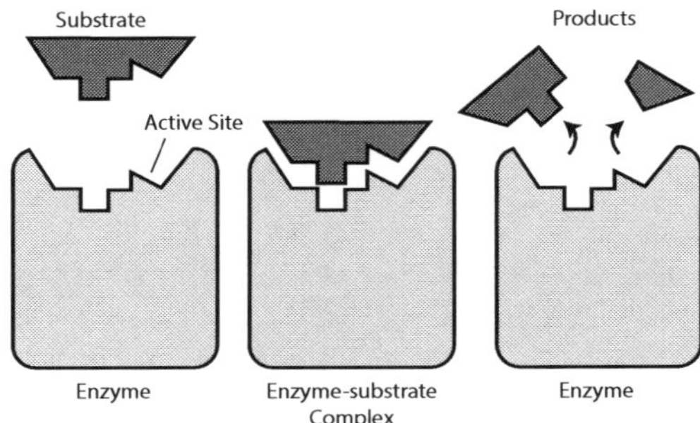

A) the enzyme

B) the enzyme-substrate complex

C) the substrate

D) the active site

51. A student wants to find information on the Battle of the Scheldt. According to the index for a history textbook, where should the student look?

Battle of San Marino	112 – 3, 201
Battle of Sedan	113, 202
Battle of Sidi Barrani	115 – 6
Battle of Someri	203 – 205
Battle of Stalingrad	306 – 310
Battle of Studzianki	307 – 308
Battle of the Scheldt	110 – 2, 207

A) 110

B) 115

C) 203

D) 307

In its most basic form, geography is the study of space; more specifically, it studies the physical space of the earth and the ways in which it interacts with, shapes, and is shaped by its habitants. Geographers look at the world from a spatial perspective. This means that at the center of all geographic study is the question, where? For geographers, the where of any interaction, event, or development is a crucial element to understanding it.

This question of where can be asked in a variety of fields of study, so there are many sub-disciplines of geography. These can be organized into four main categories: 1) regional studies, which examine the characteristics of a particular place, 2) topical studies, which look at a single physical or human feature that impacts the whole world, 3) physical studies, which focus on the physical features of Earth, and 4) human studies, which examine the relationship between human activity and the environment.

52. A researcher studying the relationship between farming and river systems would be engaged in which of the following geographical sub-disciplines?

A) regional studies

B) topical studies

C) physical studies

D) human studies

53. Which of the following best describes the mode of the passage?

A) expository

B) narrative

C) persuasive

D) descriptive

54. Which of the following is a concise summary of the passage?

A) The most important questions in geography are where an event or development took place.

B) Geography, which is the study of the physical space on earth, can be broken down into four sub-disciplines.

C) Regional studies is the study of a single region or area.

D) Geography can be broken down into four sub-disciplines: regional studies, topical studies, physical studies, and human studies.

The next three questions are based on this passage.

It's that time again—the annual Friendswood Village Summer Fair is here! Last year we had a record number of visitors, and we're expecting an even bigger turnout this year. The fair will be bringing back all our traditional food and games, including the famous raffle. This year, we'll have a carousel, petting zoo, and climbing wall (for teenagers and adults only, please). We're also excited to welcome Petey's BBQ and Happy Tummy's Frozen Treats, who are both new to the fair this year. Tickets are available online and at local retailers.

55. Which of the following will NOT be a new presence at the Fair this year?

A) the raffle

B) the petting zoo

C) the carousel

D) Petey's BBQ

56. Based on the context, which of the following is the meaning of the word *record* in the passage?

A) a piece of evidence

B) a disk with a groove that reproduces sound

C) the best or most remarkable

D) to set down in writing

57. Which of the following best describes the mode of the passage?

A) expository

B) narrative

C) persuasive

D) descriptive

CONTINUE

58. Based on the pattern in the headings, which of the following is a reasonable heading to insert in the blank spot?

> **Chapter 3. Emotions and the Central Nervous System**
>
> 3A. Involuntary Physical Symptoms of Emotion
>
>   a) Flushing
>
>   b) _______
>
>   c) Vocal Changes
>
> 3B. Voluntary Physical Response to Emotion
>
> 3C. Conscious Control of Emotions

A) Facial Expressions

B) Happiness

C) Emotions and Central Nervous System Disorders

D) The Cerebral Cortex

59. Based on the pattern in the headings, which of the following is a reasonable heading to insert in the blank spot?

> **I. Types of Teas**
>
> A.   Black Tea
>
>   a) Assam
>
>   b) Darjeeling
>
>   c) Ceylong
>
> B.   _______
>
> C.   White Tea

A) Green Tea

B) Iced Tea

C) Cold-Brew Tea

D) Chai Tea

The next two questions are based on the table of contents below.

Table of Contents

60. A student wants to find information on how the Potsdam Treaty, signed at the end of World War II, affected the Cold War. On which of the following pages will the student most likely find this information?

A) 155

B) 256

C) 308

D) 383

61. A researcher wants to find information on a movie made in 1967 about the Cold War. On which of the following pages should the researcher look for this information?

A) 168

B) 300

C) 311

D) 370

The next three questions are based on this passage.

Alexis de Tocqueville, a young Frenchman from an aristocratic family, visited the United States in the early 1800s. He observed: "Amongst the novel objects that attracted my attention during my stay in the United States, nothing struck me more forcibly than the general equality of conditions. […] The more I advanced in the study of American society, the more I perceived that the equality of conditions is the fundamental fact from which all others seem to be derived, and the central point at which all my observations constantly terminated."

Excerpt from Alexis de Tocqueville's Democracy in America, 1835

62. Which of the following best states the main idea of the passage?

A) Alexis de Tocqueville has contributed substantially to the study of the nineteenth-century United States.

B) Equality was the most important ideal in the nineteenth-century United States.

C) In nineteenth-century American society, all people had rights.

D) American society during the nineteenth century was more equal than French society.

63. Based on the context, which of the following is the meaning of the word *novel* in the passage?

A) new

B) written

C) uncertain

D) confusing

64. Which of the following is an example of a primary source that would be used in a research paper on the history of mining in West Virginia?

A) a book written by a modern historian on the growth of American unions

B) letters written by a miner to his family in New York

C) a recent documentary on historical mining equipment

D) a historical novel set in a mining camp in West Virginia

65. The author would most likely agree with which of the following statements about the United States in the nineteenth century?

A) Right from the beginning at least three social classes emerged, with most people falling in the middle.

B) American people were by nature competitive and individualistic.

C) Since the birth of the United States, its citizens have been eager to achieve and prosper.

D) In the early decades when America had just become an independent country with a new government, people lived in equality.

66. Spanish *conquistadors* explored what is today the Southwest United States, claiming land for Spain despite the presence of southwestern tribes.

Italics are used in the passage above for which of the following reasons?

A) to show that a word is intentionally misspelled

B) to indicate a word in a foreign language

C) to emphasize a contrast

D) to reference a footnote

67. The strange light in the room made it hard to determine the colors used in the painting.

Based on the context of the passage above, which of the following is the meaning of the word *light* in the sentence?

A) a sense of mental illumination or enlightenment

B) the electromagnetic waves that make human vision possible

C) a device used to indicate right of way for traffic

D) to start a fire

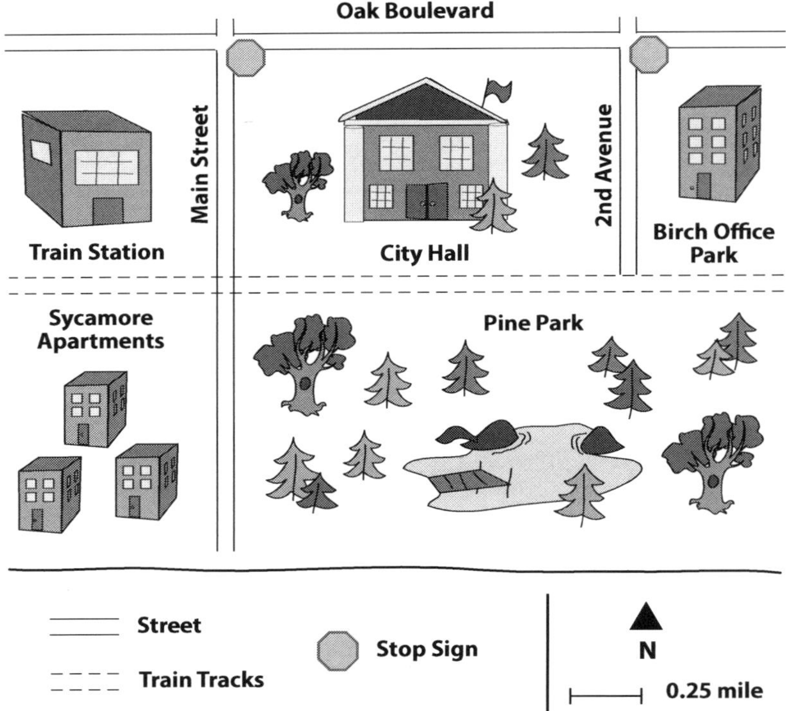

68. A family leaves the train station and heads south on Main Street. At which of the following locations will the train arrive?

A) City Hall

B) Oak Boulevard

C) Sycamore Apartments

D) Birch Office Park

69. According to the map, which of the following is the distance from City Hall to the Birch Office Park?

A) 0.1 miles

B) 1 mile

C) 10 miles

D) 100 miles

The next five questions are based on this passage.

The most important part of brewing coffee is getting the right water. Choose a water that you think has a nice, neutral flavor. Anything with too many minerals or contaminants will change the flavor of the coffee, and water with too few minerals won't do a good job of extracting the flavor from the coffee beans. Water should be heated to between 195 and 205 degrees Fahrenheit. Boiling water (212 degrees Fahrenheit) will burn the beans and give your coffee a scorched flavor.

While the water is heating, grind your beans. Remember, the fresher the grind, the fresher the flavor of the coffee. The number of beans is entirely dependent on your personal taste. Obviously, more beans will result in a more robust flavor, while fewer beans will give your coffee a more subtle taste. The texture of the grind should be not too fine (which can lead to bitter coffee) or too large (which can lead to weak coffee).

Once the beans are ground and the water has reached the perfect temperature, you're ready to brew. A French press (which we recommend), allows you to control brewing time and provide a thorough brew. Pour the grounds into the press, then pour the hot water over the grounds and let it steep. The brew shouldn't require more than 5 minutes, although those of you who like your coffee a bit harsher can leave it longer. Finally, use the plunger to remove the grounds and pour.

70. According to the passage, which of the following lists the steps for brewing coffee in the correct sequence?

A) Choose a water that doesn't have too many or two few minerals. Then, heat water to boiling and pour over coffee grounds.

B) Ground the beans to the appropriate texture and pour into the French press. Then, heat water to boiling and pour over the ground beans. Finally, use the plunger to remove the grounds and pour.

C) Ground beans to the appropriate texture, and then heat water to 195 degrees Fahrenheit. Next, pour water over the grounds and steep for no more than five minutes. Finally, remove the grounds using the plunger.

D) Choose the right type of water and heat it to the correct temperature. Next, ground the beans and put them in the French press. Then, pour the hot water over the grounds and let the coffee steep.

71. Which of the following statements based on the passage should be considered an opinion?

A) While the water is heating, grind your beans.

B) A French press (which we recommend), allows you to control brewing time and provide a thorough brew.

C) Anything with too many minerals or contaminants will change the flavor of the coffee, and water with too few minerals won't do a good job of extracting the flavor from the coffee beans.

D) Finally, use the plunger to remove the grounds and pour.

72. Which of the following best describes the structure of the text?

A) chronological

B) cause and effect

C) problem and solution

D) contrast

73. Which of the following conclusions is best supported by the passage?

A) Coffee should never be brewed for longer than 5 minutes.

B) It's better to use too many coffee beans when making coffee than too few.

C) Brewing quality coffee at home is too complicated for most people to do well.

D) The best way to brew coffee is often determined by personal preferences.

74. Which of the following would be an appropriate title for this passage?

A) How to Brew the Perfect Cup of Coffee

B) Why Drinking Coffee Is the Best Way to Start the Day

C) How to Use a French Press to Make Coffee

D) The Importance of Grinding Coffee Beans

The next two questions are based on this passage.

For an adult person to be unable to swim points to something like criminal negligence; every man, woman and child should learn. A person who cannot swim may not only become a danger to himself, but to someone, and perhaps to several, of his fellow beings. Children as early as the age of four may acquire the art; none are too young, none too old.

Frank Eugen Dalton, *Swimming Scientifically Taught*, 1912

75. Which of the following best captures the author's purpose?

  A) to encourage the reader to learn to swim

  B) to explain how people who cannot swim are a danger to others

  C) to inform the reader that it's never too late to learn to swim

  D) to argue that people who cannot swim should be punished

76. Which of the following is the purpose of this passage?

  A) to inform

  B) to entertain

  C) to describe

  D) to persuade

The next three questions are based on this passage.

New Policy for Replacement Student Identification Cards

Due to recent issues with the abuse of student identification (ID) cards, Campus Security has issued a new policy for acquiring replacement student identification cards.

The following conditions must be met for students to receive a replacement student ID card:

◆   Student is currently enrolled in at least one class; the class may be either online or on campus.

◆   Student must have been issued a student ID card within the last five years.

◆   Student must apply for a replacement ID card in person at the Student Admissions Office. Online applications will no longer be accepted.

◆   Students will be required to pay a $25 fee for each replacement ID card. Fee may not be charged to the student's account.

Students who do not meet these conditions will be required to apply for a new ID card at the Campus Security Office.

77. Based on the context, which of the following is the meaning of the word *abuse* in the passage?

  A) failure

  B) punishment

  C) misuse

  D) disappearance

78. Which of the following would not be eligible to receive a replacement student ID card from the Student Admissions Office?

  A) a student enrolled in one online class

  B) a student who lives abroad and must apply for her replacement student ID online

  C) a currently enrolled student who has lost his student ID card

  D) a student who has reenrolled after a three year absence from the school

79. Which of the following best describes the purpose of this passage?

  A) to ensure that students pay the appropriate fee when applying for a replacement ID card

  B) to inform students of the new policy regarding replacement ID cards

  C) to inform online students that they will no longer be eligible to receive replacement ID cards

  D) to punish students who have used student ID cards incorrectly in the past

The next three questions are based on this passage.

Alfie closed his eyes and took several deep breaths. He was trying to ignore the sounds of the crowd, but even he had to admit that it was hard not to notice the tension in the stadium. He could feel 50,000 sets of eyes burning through his skin—this crowd expected perfection from him. He took another breath and opened his eyes, setting his sights on the soccer ball resting peacefully in the grass. One shot, just one last shot, between his team and the championship. He didn't look up at the goalie, who was jumping nervously on the goal line just a few yards away. Afterward, he would swear he didn't remember anything between the referee's whistle and the thunderous roar of the crowd.

80. Which of the following conclusions is best supported by the passage?

   A) Alfie passed out on the field and was unable to take the shot.

   B) The goalie blocked Alfie's shot.

   C) Alfie scored the goal and won his team the championship.

   D) The referee declared the game a tie.

81. Which of the following best describes the meaning of the phrase "he could feel 50,000 sets of eyes burning through his skin"?

   A) The 50,000 people in the stadium were trying to hurt Alfie.

   B) Alfie felt uncomfortable and exposed in front of my so many people.

   C) Alfie felt immense pressure from the 50,000 people watching him.

   D) The people in the stadium are warning Alfie that the field is on fire.

82. Which of the following indicates the beginning of a sequence?

   A) Although she was initially apprehensive about the class, she soon grew to enjoy it.

   B) Before he decided what to order for dinner, he had to decide on a restaurant.

   C) At the moment, I can think of nothing more wonderful than a glass of lemonade.

   D) To begin the restoration, they tore out the rotten floorboards.

83. Which of the following best describes the mode of the passage?

   A) expository

   B) narrative

   C) persuasive

   D) descriptive

84. Start with the shapes shown below. Follow the directions.

1. Move triangle 1 to the right of triangle 3.
2. Swap triangles 2 and 3.
3. Rotate triangle 6 180 degrees.
4. Swap triangles 4 and 1.

Which of the following shows the order in which the shapes now appear?

A)

B)

C)

D)

> Hannah —
>
> Congratulations on the promotion! I just heard the news from the receptionist in Accounting—she says you're already packing up to move into your big new office.
>
> Before you make the official move to upper management, I'd like to make sure we get proper documentation in place for your replacement. (You remember what a pain it was when you trained a few years ago.) To that end, could you please make a list of your current job responsibilities and include a list of all currently available training material that will be necessary for the person who takes over that job? If you feel new training documents are necessary, please include a description of these, and I'll have someone type them up for you.
>
> Congratulations again—you've earned it.
>
> Best regards,
>
> Sasha

85. Which of the following best captures the author's purpose?

   A) to inform Hannah that the receptionist in Accounting is telling people about her promotion

   B) to let Hannah know she has performed well at work despite not receiving good training

   C) to congratulate Hannah on her promotion

   D) to acquire information from Hannah in order to train her replacement

86. Which of the following best describes the relationship of the writer to Hannah?

   A) Hannah's manager

   B) Hannah's coworker

   C) Hannah's friend

   D) Hannah's replacement

The next two questions are based on the passage below.

East River High School has released its graduation summary for the class of 2016. Out of a total of 558 senior students, 525 (94 percent) successfully completed their degree program and graduated. Of these, 402 (representing 72 percent of the total class) went on to attend to a two- or four-year college or university. The distribution of students among the four main types of colleges and universities—small or large private and small or large public—is shown in the corresponding figure. As the data shows, the majority of East River High School's college-attending graduates chose a large, public institution.

87. According to the figure, how many students from East River High School will attend a small, public college or university?

   A) 4

   B) 44

   C) 440

   D) 4400

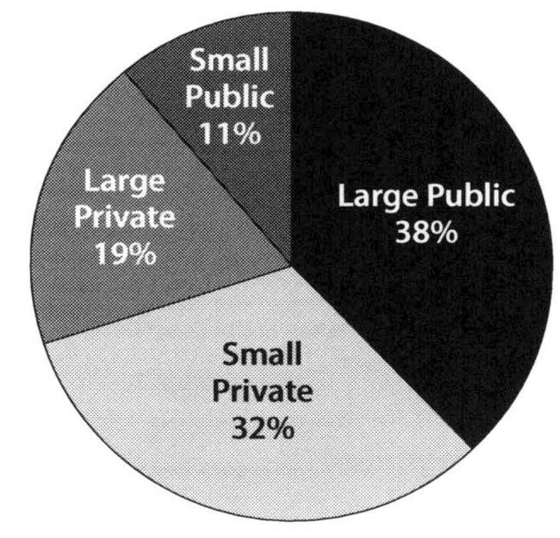

88. Which of the following best describes the tone of the passage?

   A) professional

   B) casual

   C) concerned

   D) congratulatory

89. A man is examining cake recipes to find one that will be suitable for his friend, who cannot eat dairy products. According the lists of required ingredients, which of the following should he choose?

   A) Recipe Ingredients – flour, sugar, water, milk, eggs, baking powder, baking soda, chocolate powder, almonds

   B) Recipe Ingredients – cake flour, vegetable oil, butter, eggs, baking powder, chocolate chips

   C) Recipe Ingredients – flour, brown sugar, butter, eggs, baking soda, vanilla extract, macadamia nuts

   D) Recipe Ingredients – flour, sugar, brown sugar, vegetable oil, eggs, applesauce, baking powder, vanilla extract

90. A student has written the paragraph below as an introduction to a paper. Which of the following is most likely the topic of the paper?

It has now been two decades since the introduction of thermonuclear fusion weapons into the military inventories of the great powers, and more than a decade since the United States, Great Britain, and the Soviet Union ceased to test nuclear weapons in the atmosphere. Today our understanding of the technology of thermonuclear weapons seems highly advanced, but our knowledge of the physical and biological consequences of nuclear war is continuously evolving.

United States Arms Control and Disarmament Agency, Worldwide Effects of Nuclear War: Some Perspectives, 1998

   A) the impact of thermonuclear weapons on the military

   B) the technology of thermonuclear weapons

   C) atmospheric testing of nuclear weapons

   D) the physical and biological consequences of nuclear war

The next two questions are based on this passage.

Ms. Rodriguez —

A recent review of our accounts has shown that you were mistakenly overcharged for your October water bill. Due to a system error, customers in your area were charged twice for their October water usage. We regret the error, and are currently in the process of issuing refunds using the following criteria:

- Customers who paid with a debit card or bank account will receive refunds directly deposited into their bank accounts.
- Credit card transactions will be canceled by our company and will not appear on your statement.
- Customer who paid via check will receive a refund check in the mail in 4 – 6 weeks.

Your business is important to us, and we value your continued support. To demonstrate our commitment to our customers, we will be offering a 5% discount during the month of November to customers affected by this accounting error.

Please contact me directly if you have any questions about your bill or the refund process.

Regards,

Timothy Halgren

Director, Customer Relations
Greenway Water Company

---

91. Which of the following best describes the
purpose of the passage?

   A) to inform customers that they will
   receive a 5% discount on their water
   bills during the month of November

   B) to inform customers that they were
   overcharged and will be receiving
   refunds

   C) to urge customers to contact their
   customer service representatives with
   questions about their bills

   D) to thank customers for their continued
   support

92. Which of the following conclusions is well
supported by the passage?

   A) Greenway Water Company will soon go
   out of business when customers leave.

   B) Ms. Rodriguez will receive a refund
   check in the mail in 4 – 6 weeks.

   C) Greenway Water Company is concerned
   that customers may be upset by the
   error.

   D) All customers of Greenway Water
   Company will receive refunds for being
   overcharged in October.

The next two questions are based on the index below.

New Zealand .... 125 – 127, 212 – 215, 306

Nicaragua.. 76, 132 – 151

Niger... 15 – 22, 317 – 320

Nigeria ....16 – 18, 246

North Korea ....101 – 105, 221 – 231, 313

Norway... 135 – 140, 295

93. A student wants to find information on the
Oslo, the capital of Norway. According the
index for a geography book, where should
the student look first?

   A) 15

   B) 125

   C) 135

   D) 221

94. A student wants to find information on
rivers in Niger. According the index for a
geography book, where should the student
look first?

   A) 15

   B) 101

   C) 212

   D) 313

The next three questions are based on this passage.

We've been told for years that the recipe for weight loss is fewer calories in than calories out. In other
words, eat less and exercise more, and your body will take care of the rest. As many of those who've tried
to diet can attest, this edict doesn't always produce results. If you're one of those folks, you might have felt
that you just weren't doing it right—that the failure was all your fault.

However, several new studies released this year have suggested that it might not be your fault at
all. For example, a study of people who'd lost a high percentage of their body weight (>17%) in a short
period of time found that they could not physically maintain their new weight. Scientists measured
their resting metabolic rate and found that they'd need to consume only a few hundred calories a
day to meet their metabolic needs. Basically, their bodies were in starvation mode and seemed to
desperately hang on to each and every calorie. Eating even a single healthy, well-balanced meal a
day would cause these subjects to start packing back on the pounds.

Other studies have shown that factors like intestinal bacteria, distribution of body fat, and hormone
levels can affect the manner in which our bodies process calories. There's also the fact that it's actually

quite difficult to measure the number of calories consumed during a particular meal and the number used while exercising.

95. Which of the following would be the best summary statement to conclude the passage?

A) It turns out that conventional dieting wisdom doesn't capture the whole picture of how our bodies function.

B) Still, counting calories and tracking exercise is a good idea if you want to lose weight.

C) In conclusion, it's important to lose weight responsibly: losing too much weight at once can negatively impact the body.

D) It's easy to see that diets don't work, so we should focus less on weight loss and more on overall health.

96. Which of the following type of arguments is used in the passage?

A) emotional argument

B) appeal to authority

C) specific evidence

D) rhetorical questioning

97. Which of the following would weaken the author's argument?

A) a new diet pill from a pharmaceutical company that promises to help patients lose weight by changing intestinal bacteria

B) the personal experience of a man who was able to lose a significant amount of weight taking in fewer calories than he used

C) a study showing that people in different geographic locations lose different amounts of weight when on the same diet

D) a study showing that people often misreport their food intake when part of a scientific study on weight loss

The next two questions are based on this chart.

Table 1.2. Prices of Office Supplies

MANUFACTURER	SHIPPING AND HANDLING
Discount Office Supplies	$0.99 per pound
Paper Clips & Staples	$12.99 flat fee for all packages
Quick & Fast Office Supplies	$7.99 flat fee for all packages under 10 pounds; $1.99 per additional pound
Blanchard Supplies	free shipping on packages under 10 pounds; $15.99 flat fee for all packages over 10 pounds

98. A company is planning ordering office supplies that will weigh 22 pounds. Based on the pricing chart, which of the following manufacturers would offer the lowest cost for shipping and handling?

A) Discount Office Supplies

B) Paper Clips & Staples

C) Quick & Fast Office Supplies

D) Blanchard Supplies

99. A company is placing an order for office supplies that will weigh 11 pounds. Based on the pricing chart, which of the following manufacturers would offer the lowest cost for shipping and handling?

A) Discount Office Supplies

B) Paper Clips & Staples

C) Quick & Fast Office Supplies

D) Blanchard Supplies

The next two questions are based on this passage.

American Cowslip: This plant grows spontaneously in Virginia and other parts of North America. It flowers in the beginning of May, and the seeds ripen in July, soon after which the stalks and leaves decay, so that the roots remain inactive till the following spring. It is propagated by offsets, which the roots put out freely when they are in a loose moist soil and a shady situation; the best time to remove the roots, and take away the offsets, is in August, after the leaves and stalks are decayed, that they may be fixed well in their new situation before the frost comes on.

William Curtis, The Botanical Magazine, 1790

100. According to the passage, which of the following is the best time to remove the roots of American Cowslip?

A) August

B) May

C) July

D) December

101. Which of the following is the meaning of *propagated* as used in the sentence?

A) killed

B) multiplied

C) extracted

D) concealed

102. According to the figure below, which of the following is a difference between pyrimidine and purine bases?

Cytosine C   Thymine T

pyrimidine bases

Adenine A   Guanine G

purine bases

A) Pyrimidine bases do not include an amine group (NH$_2$), while purine bases do.

B) Pyrimidine bases have an oxygen atom, while purine bases do not.

C) Pyrimidine bases have a single carbon nitrogen ring, while purine bases have two.

D) Pyrimidine bases are found in DNA and RNA, while purine bases are found only in DNA.

103. Which of the following represents the temperature in degrees Fahrenheit according to the thermometer above?

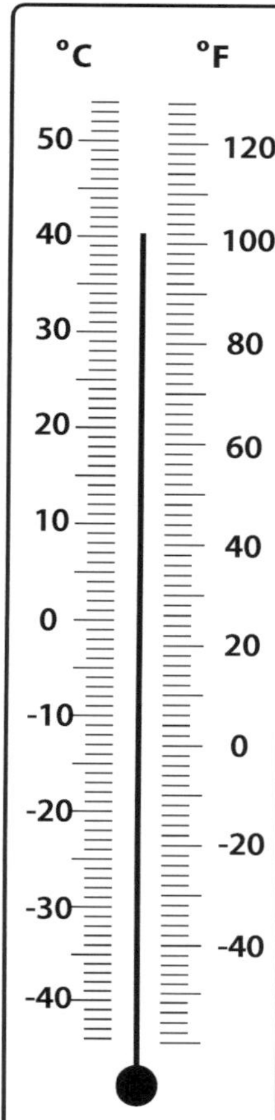

A) −10

B) 48

C) 54

D) 76

104. Based on the pattern in the headings, which of the following is a reasonable heading to insert in the blank spot?

> **5. The Human Digestive System**
>   A. The Digestive Tract
>   1) Mouth
>   2) Esophagus
>   3) __________
>   4) Intestines
>   B. Accessory Organs
>   1) Salivary Glands
>   2) Liver
>   3) Gall Bladder

A) Stomach

B) Pancreas

C) Heart

D) Proteins

ANSWER KEY

1. **B) is correct.** The purpose of the passage is to explain what an idealist believes in. The author does not offer any opinions or try to persuade readers about the importance of certain values.

2. **A) is correct.** The systolic blood pressure is the higher number marked as "Sys" on the monitor.

3. **D) is correct.** The loyal dog is presented in contrast with humans, who are not always trustworthy or faithful.

4. **A) is correct.** The author is describing the constancy of dogs as friends. He concludes by stating, "When all other friends desert, he [a dog] remains."

5. **C) is correct.** The passage emphasizes that people can be treacherous, but a dog will be a constant friend. The passage does not suggest that relationships with other people are pointless or useless.

6. **D) is correct.** The author is trying to persuade his audience that dogs are loyal friends.

7. **B) is correct.** The first step in the *After Planting* section is to water the plants immediately.

8. **A) is correct.** In the *Before Planting* section, the directions say to mix in fertilizer or compost after the soil has been loosened.

9. **C) is correct.** The author and Alan have a friendly relationship, as evidenced by the author's casual tone and his offer to bring Alan a gift from his vacation.

10. **C) is correct.** The author is writing to tell Alan that he will be out of the office. The details about his trip and the meeting support this idea.

11. **B) is correct.** The Scout Camp is due north of the Fire Circle.

12. **A) is correct.** The Old Oak Tree lies on the trail between the Fishing Pond and the Fire Circle.

13. **D) is correct.** The author wants to bring customers into Carl's Car Depot, doing so by highlighting the low prices and range of cars available.

14. **B) is correct.** The word *sell* best describes the author's implication that the cars are priced to be sold quickly.

15. **A) is correct.** The passage does not mention warranties.

16. **C) is correct.** The word *said* is italicized to provide emphasis and contrast with the word actions.

17. **A) is correct.** Choice A describes the order of Julia's actions that matches chronological order of the passage.

18. **B) is correct.** The passage describes how Julia had an exhausting morning, and it can be assumed that when "she'd had enough" she decided to go home.

19. **C) is correct.** Whether or not it was irresponsible for Julia to leave work is a matter of opinion. Some readers may agree, and others may disagree. The other statements are facts that can be proven from the passage.

20. **B) is correct.** The phrase "set a course for home" is an idiom that means to head in a certain direction, so Julia is planning to go home.

21. **D) is correct.** The passage emphasizes that Julia is tired, so she's most likely to drive home and go to sleep.

22. **D) is correct.** In the passage, Thomas Jefferson is defined as an anti-Federalist, in contrast with Federalists who believe in a strong federal government.

23. **B) is correct.** *Tropical Frogs* belongs under the heading *Frogs* with the other types of frogs. The blank spot should not include a specific type of frog or refer to amphibians other than frogs.

24. **A) is correct.** Only Choice A is a source produced by someone who does not have first-hand experience of World War I.

25. **A) is correct.** Victoria's win implies that she played in a competitive event.

26. **D) is correct.** Quarter Price Books has the lowest price:
$(3.99 \times 25) + (2.99 \times 50) = 249.25$

27. **B) is correct.** The Book Barn would offer the lowest price: $98 for twenty-five books.

28. **A) is correct.** A company that profits from private tutoring might introduce bias into a study on the effects of private tutoring in schools.

29. **C) is correct.** The author cites data from a study to support his or her argument.

30. **C) is correct.** Choice C shows the correct order of the blocks after following the directions.

31. **D) is correct.** Choice D correctly lists the houses the author visited as listed chronologically in the passage.

32. **B) is correct.** The author says that the house on Pine Street "had enough space inside but didn't have a big enough yard for our three dogs."

33. **B) is correct.** A local paper is the source most likely to provide an unbiased assessment of the candidates in a state election.

34. **D) is correct.** The passage concludes with the statement "our Human Resources team will be taking longer than previously stated to review candidates and schedule interviews" and a time window in which Mr. Morgan can expect to receive feedback.

35. **A) is correct.** The author of the passage states that the team will be taking "longer than previously stated," implying that she had previously told Mr. Morgan that the process would take less than two weeks.

36. **C) is correct.** The passage states that babies' senses are much like those of their adult counterparts with the exception of their vision, which develops later.

37. **B) is correct.** The passage states that "infants rely primarily on hearing."

38. **A) is correct.** The passage explains how a baby's senses develop and allow it to interact with the world.

39. **C) is correct.** Ginger appears on the list for fall.

40. **B) is correct.** *Lamb* fits best with the pattern of subheadings naming specific types of meat.

41. **B) is correct.** Only Choice B includes the fact that both Epimetheus and Prometheus were assigned to create living things; it then clarifies that Epimetheus gave positive traits to animals, while Prometheus gave fire to humans. This choice includes all the important parts of the passage without adding other emotions or details.

42. **D) is correct.** The word *given* best describes the idea that the gifts have been handed out.

43. **A) is correct.** Page 55 is included in the section on Italian painters.

44. **C) is correct.** Page 153 is the beginning of the section on High Renaissance architecture, which includes the year 1518.

45. **B) is correct.** In February the service earned $1100, and in April it earned $200. The difference between the two months is $900.

46. **B) is correct.** The author uses several markers of casual writing, including the first person, exclamation marks, and informal language.

47. **D) is correct.** The passage states that restaurateurs must be "exact and ruthless with their budget and pricing." The success of The Hot Dog implies that its owners have done that.

48. **D) is correct.** *Evidence* best describes the idea that The Hot Dog's longevity is proof of its owners' skills.

49. **C) is correct.** The transition word *finally* indicates that it is the end of a sequence.

50. **C) is correct.** The diagram indicates that products are formed when the substrate is broken apart.

51. **A) is correct.** The index shows that the Battle of the Scheldt appears on page 110.

52. **D) is correct.** The passage describes human studies as the study of "the relationship between human activity and the environment," which would include farmers interacting with river systems.

53. **A) is correct.** The passage explains what the study of geography involves and outlines its main sub-disciplines.

54. **B) is correct.** Only this choice summarizes the two main points of the passage: the definition of geography and the breakdown of its sub-disciplines.

55. **A) is correct.** The raffle is the only feature described as an event the organizers will be "bringing back."

56. **C) is correct.** The "record number of visitors" is the highest, or best, number of visitors to the fair.

57. **C) is correct.** The passage is trying to persuade people to attend the Friendswood Village Summer Fair.

58. **A) is correct.** Only "Facial Expressions" fits with the other subheadings under the category "Involuntary Physical Symptoms of Emotion."

59. **A) is correct.** Only *Green Tea* fits the pattern of headings that describe categories of tea based on color.

60. **A) is correct.** Page 155 is included in the section that covers the end of World War II.

61. **C) is correct.** Page 311 is included in the section on depictions of the Cold War in popular culture between 1945 and 1991.

62. **B) is correct.** The author notes de Tocqueville's observation: "The more I advanced in the study of American society, the more I perceived that the equality of conditions is the fundamental fact from which all others seem to be derived," implying that equality was the most important ideal in the United States.

63. **A) is correct.** *New* best describes the idea that the writer is encountering things he has never seen before.

64. **D) is correct.** "Equality of conditions" suggests that people's living conditions, in terms of economics and social status, were equal.

65. **B) is correct.** Letters from a first-hand witness would be a primary source.

66. **B) is correct.** The word *conquistadors* is italicized to indicate it is in a foreign language.

67. **B) is correct.** The fact that the light is affecting how a painting is viewed implies that the word light is being used to describe the electromagnetic waves that make human vision possible.

68. **C) is correct.** Of the four choices, only Sycamore Apartments is located on Main Street south of the train station.

69. **B) is correct.** The scale shows that the two buildings are approximately 1 mile apart.

70. **D) is correct.** This choice lists the steps for brewing coffee in the same order as the passage.

71. **B) is correct.** The writer uses the first person, showing his or her opinion, to recommend a French press as the best way to brew coffee.

72. **A) is correct.** The author describes the steps for making coffee in chronological order.

73. **D) is correct.** The passage mentions several times that decisions about things like water minerals, ground size, and steep time will depend on the preference of the coffee drinker.

74. **A) is correct.** The passage as a whole describes from start to finish how to make a cup of coffee the drinker will enjoy.

75. **A) is correct.** The author argues that "every man, woman and child should learn" to swim, and then explains to the reader why he or she should be able to swim.

76. **D) is correct.** The author wants to persuade the reader that swimming is a necessary skill.

77. **C) is correct.** *Misuse* best describes the passage's implication that student ID cards have been used incorrectly or fraudulently.

78. **B) is correct.** The new policy states that the "student must apply for a replacement ID card in person at the Student Admissions Office. Online applications will no longer be accepted."

79. **B) is correct.** As shown in the title and opening sentence, the passage is written to inform students about changes to the policy.

80. **C) is correct.** The crowd's support for Alfie and their collective roar after the shot implies that Alfie scored the goal and won the championship.

81. **C) is correct.** The metaphor implies that Alfie felt pressure from the people watching him to perform well. There is no indication that he is threatened physically.

82. **D) is correct.** This statement starts with the phrase *to begin*, which introduces a series or sequence.

83. **B) is correct.** The passage is narrative, meaning it tells a story.

84. **A) is correct.** Choice A shows the correct order and placement of the triangles after following the directions.

85. **D) is correct.** While the passage opens with a congratulatory message, the main purpose of the passage is to ask for a list of job responsibilities and training materials from Hannah.

86. **B) is correct.** The tone and content of the passage implies that the writer is a coworker of Hannah's. She is likely not her manager, since she just learned of the promotion. She is also not the replacement, since she is planning to train that person in the future.

87. **B) is correct.** The passage states that 402 students went on to attend college or university, and 11 percent of 402 is approximately 44 students.

88. **A) is correct.** The passage is written in a neutral, professional tone. It does not include any informal, emotional, or first-person language.

89. **D) is correct.** Only this recipe does not include milk or butter, both of which are dairy products.

90. **D) is correct.** The passage gives a short history of thermonuclear weapons and then introduces its main topic—the physical and biological consequences of nuclear war.

91. **B) is correct.** The main purpose of the passage is to inform customers about the accounting error and to let them know how they will receive their refunds.

92. **C) is correct.** The company ends the passage by expressing its appreciation for customers and offering both a discount and a personal contact within the company, implying it is trying to improve customer relations.

93. **C) is correct.** The index shows that page 135 is the first mention of Norway in the book.

94. **A) is correct.** The index shows that page 15 is the first mention of Niger in the book.

95. **A) is correct.** The bulk of the passage is dedicated to showing that conventional wisdom about "fewer calories in than calories out" isn't true for many people and is more complicated than previously believed.

96. **C) is correct.** The author cites several scientific studies to support the argument.

97. **D) is correct.** People misreporting the amount of food they ate would introduce error into studies on weight loss and might make the studies the author cites unreliable.

98. **B) is correct.** Paper Clips & Staples offers the cheapest shipping and handling cost for a 22-pound package.

99. **C) is correct.** Quick & Fast Office Supplies offers the cheapest shipping and handling cost for an 11-pound package: $7.99 + (1.99 \times 1) = \$9.98$.

100. **A) is correct.** The passage states that "the best time to remove the roots, and take away the offsets, is in August."

101. **B) is correct.** *Multiplied* best describes the passage's description of how the plant reproduces by producing offsets.

102. **C) is correct.** The figure shows that pyrimidines have a single carbon nitrogen ring, while purines have two.

103. **C) is correct.** 12 degrees F (Fahrenheit) corresponds to 54 degrees C (Celsius) on the thermometer's scale.

104. **A) is correct.** The stomach is the only choice that is an organ in the human digestive tract.

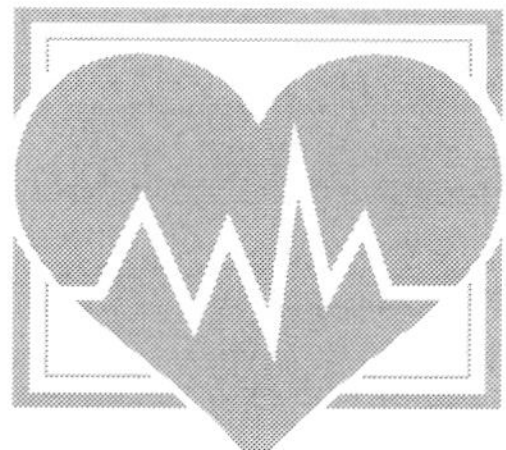

SCIENCE

Directions: Read the question carefully, and choose the best answer.

1. Which of the following describes the primary function of the respiratory system?

   A) to create sound and speech

   B) to take oxygen into the body while removing carbon dioxide

   C) to transport nutrients to the cells and tissue of the body

   D) to act as a barrier between the body's organs and outside influences

2. Which of the following is the first step of the scientific method?

   A) construct a hypothesis

   B) make observations

   C) analyze data

   D) form a question

3. The process of organisms with an advantageous trait surviving more often and producing more offspring than organisms without the advantageous trait describes which of the following basic mechanisms of evolution?

   A) gene flow

   B) genetic drift

   C) mutation

   D) natural selection

4. Which of the following is the group of basophils that produces follicle-stimulating hormone (FSH) and luteinizing hormone (LH)?

   A) gonadotrophs

   B) thyrotroph

   C) chromophil

   D) pituicytes

5. Which of the following are considered the basic units of the female reproductive system, each containing a single immature egg cell that is released during ovulation?

   A) oocytes

   B) follicles

   C) ovaries

   D) fundus

6. Which of the following describes the muscular organ that processes food material into increasingly smaller pieces, mixes it with saliva to create a bolus, and creates a barrier to transport food into the esophagus?

   A) pharynx

   B) tongue

   C) diaphragm

   D) stomach

7. Which of the following chambers of the heart receives blood returning from the lungs during pulmonary circulation?

   A) left atrium

   B) right atrium

   C) left ventricle

   D) right ventricle

8. Which of the following is the lobe in the cerebral cortex primarily responsible for processing and integrating sensory information received from the rest of the body?

   A) frontal lobe

   B) occipital lobe

   C) parietal lobe

   D) temporal lobe

9. Which of the following is an example of adaptive, or specific, immunity?

   A) inflammation

   B) fever

   C) humoral

   D) phagocytosis

10. Which of the following describes a situation in which research results are consistent with every subsequent experiment, but the test used in the experiment does not measure what it claims to measure?

   A) reliable, but not valid

   B) valid, but not reliable

   C) neither reliable nor valid

   D) both reliable and valid

11. Which of the following Mendellian laws describes how pairs of alleles within genes separate and recombine separately from other genes?

   A) law of segregation

   B) law of dominance

   C) law of independent assortment

   D) law of predictive traits

12. Which of the following describes how atomic radius varies across the periodic table?

   A) Atomic radius increases from top to bottom and left to right on the periodic table.

   B) Atomic radius increases from top to bottom and right to left on the periodic table.

   C) Atomic radius increases from top to bottom and toward the halogens on the periodic table.

   D) Atomic radius increases from top to bottom and toward the noble gases on the periodic table.

13. Which of the following is NOT a tissue layer found in skeletal bone?

   A) periosteum

   B) bone marrow

   C) enamel

   D) cancellous bone

14. Which of the following sets of valves is primarily responsible for preventing blood flow from major blood vessels to the heart?

   A) atrioventricular valves

   B) semilunar valves

   C) tricuspid valves

   D) bicuspid valves

15. Bone is composed primarily of which of the following inorganic materials?

   A) calcium

   B) magnesium

   C) collagen

   D) potassium

16. Which of the following is the primary physical barrier the body uses to prevent infection?

   A) mucus membranes

   B) stomach acid

   C) skin

   D) urine

17. Which of the following is the connective area where nerve impulses send neurotransmitters across a synapse to a muscle cell to stimulate muscle contraction?

A) sarcomere

B) tendon

C) nicotinic receptors

D) neuromuscular junction

18. Which of the following is the region of the brain that controls and regulates autonomic functions such as respiration, digestion, and heart rate?

A) cerebellum

B) medulla oblongata

C) temporal lobe

D) cerebral cortex

19. Which of the following describes the primary function of the pyloric sphincter?

A) to regulate the movement of digested food material from the stomach to the duodenum

B) to neutralize stomach acid

C) to prevent food materials and stomach acid from leaking into other bodily tissues

D) to begin the process of chemical digestion

20. Which of the following is the location of fertilization in the female?

A) uterus

B) fallopian tube

C) endometrium

D) fimbriae

21. The pineal gland is located in which of the following areas in the body?

A) below the larynx

B) above the kidney

C) at the center of the brain hemispheres

D) at the base of the brain

22. Which of the following processes aids scientists in observing a population sample in order to answer questions about the whole population?

A) univariate analysis

B) inferential statistics

C) descriptive statistics

D) probability

23. Which of the following biological macromolecules is non-soluble, composed of hydrocarbons, and acts as an important source of energy storage for the body?

A) carbohydrates

B) nucleic acids

C) lipids

D) proteins

24. Which of the following is specialized tissue in the right atrium that acts as the heart's natural pacemaker by generating the electrical signal for the heartbeat?

A) sinus venosus

B) sinoatrial node

C) atrioventricular node

D) septa

25. Which of the following is a dense, interconnected mass of nerve cells located outside of the central nervous system?

A) ganglion

B) dendrite

C) cranial nerve

D) pons

26. Which of the following is the primary cell found in the tract of the small intestine?

A) surface absorptive cells

B) surface lining cells

C) parietal cells

D) hepatocytes

28. Which of the following describes the
general function of cytokines in the
immune system?

   A) They communicate between cells to
instigate an immune response.

   B) They inhibit blood clotting during
inflammation responses.

   C) They bind to specific pathogens to
increase pathogen mass.

   D) They transport pathogens trapped in
mucus to be destroyed in the stomach.

29. Which of the following describes the path
through which air moves during inhalation?

   A) mouth/nose > pharynx > larynx >
trachea > bronchi > bronchioles >
alveoli

   B) bronchioles > alveoli > bronchi > larynx
> pharynx > lungs

   C) mouth/nose > bronchi > bronchioles >
alveoli > lungs > trachea

   D) alveoli > bronchioles > lungs > bronchi
> trachea > larynx > pharynx > mouth/
nose

30. Which of the following is not a function of
progesterone in the female reproductive
system?

   A) expression of secondary sexual
characteristics, such as enlarged breasts

   B) stimulation of milk production in the
breasts

   C) regulation and preparation of the
endometrial lining of the uterus for
potential pregnancy

   D) inhibition of contractions of the uterus
as the ovum is released

31. Which of the following layers of skin acts
as an energy reserve by storing adipocytes
and releasing them into circulation when
energy is needed?

   A) epidermis

   B) dermis

   C) hypodermis

   D) stratum basale

32. Neurotransmitters send chemical messages
across the gap between one neuron
and another in which of the following
structures?

   A) cell membrane

   B) ganglion

   C) synapse

   D) axon

33. Hund's rule states which of the following?

   A) Chemical bonds are formed only
between electrons with similar spin.

   B) The attraction between electrons holds
atoms together.

   C) A ground state atom always has a
completely filled valence shell.

   D) Electrons fill orbitals singly and with
similar spin before pairing.

34. Which of the following is the primary
function of the large intestine?

   A) absorbing digested material into the
blood

   B) nutrient processing and metabolizing

   C) absorbing water and compacting
material into solid waste

   D) bile production and storage

The next three questions are based on the following passage.

A scientist designs an experiment to test the hypothesis that exposure to more sunlight will increase
the growth rate of elodea, a type of aquatic plant. The scientist has accumulated data from previous
experiments that identify the average growth rate of elodea exposed to natural sunlight in the wild.

In the experiment set up, there are three tanks housing ten elodea each. Tank A is positioned in front
of a window to receive natural sunlight similar to what elodea are exposed to; tank B is positioned in front
of the same window but has an additional sunlight-replicating lamp affixed to it; and tank C is positioned
in a dark corner with no exposure to natural sunlight.

35. When setting up the above experiment, the scientist has the option of using a separate water filter for each of the three tanks or using a single filtration system that attaches all three and affects them simultaneously. Which of the following filter set ups makes a more valid experiment and why?

A) separate filters for each of the three tanks, because this ensures a higher quality of water for each tank

B) one filtration system for all three tanks, because this makes filtration a controlled variable

C) one filtration system for all three tanks, because this reduces the workload for the researcher

D) separate filters for each of the three tanks, because this adds another variable to be tested and analyzed for inclusion in the experiment's results

36. The above experimental design description is an example of which of the following types of experiments?

A) field experiment

B) natural experiment

C) controlled experiment

D) observational study

37. Which of the following is the control group in the above experiment?

A) tank A

B) tank B

C) tank C

D) There is no control group in this experiment.

38. Which of the following is a type of white blood cell that plays a key role in adaptive immunity by seeking out, attacking, and destroying targeted pathogens?

A) B cells

B) goblet cells

C) antibodies

D) T cells

39. Which of the following are the blood vessels that transport blood to the heart?

A) arteries

B) capillaries

C) venules

D) veins

40. Which of the following cell organelles are the site of lipid synthesis?

A) smooth endoplasmic reticulum

B) ribosome

C) rough endoplasmic reticulum

D) Golgi apparatus

41. Which of the following describes a series of measurements that produces exact results on a consistent basis?

A) accurate

B) precise

C) valid

D) significant

42. Chromatids divide into identical chromosomes and migrate to opposite ends of the cell in which of the following phases of mitosis?

A) metaphase

B) anaphase

C) prophase

D) telophase

43. A series of muscle contractions that transports food down the digestive tract in a wave-like fashion describes which of the following?

A) digestion

B) deglutition

C) defecation

D) peristalsis

44. Which of the following is NOT a function of
the liver?

   A) nutrient processing

   B) blood filtration and detoxification

   C) cholesterol and lipoprotein production

   D) insulin production and blood sugar
   regulation

45. $2C_6H_{14} + 19O_2 \rightarrow 12CO_2 + 14H_2O$

   The reaction above is an example of which
   of the following?

   A) substitution reaction

   B) acid-base reaction

   C) enzyme reaction

   D) combustion reaction

46. Which of the following are regions of
the digestive system in which amylase is
produced?

   A) pancreas and salivary glands

   B) gall bladder and salivary glands

   C) gall bladder and liver

   D) pancreas and liver

47. Which of the following describes a cell's
reaction to being placed in a hypertonic
solution?

   A) The cell will shrink as water is
   pulled out of the cell to equalize the
   concentrations inside and outside of the
   cell.

   B) The cell will swell as water is pulled into
   the cell to equalize the concentrations
   inside and outside of the cell.

   C) The cell will remain the same size since
   the concentrations inside and outside
   the cell are equal to begin with.

   D) The pH inside the cell will drop in order
   to equalize the pH inside and outside
   the cell.

48. Which of the following are the two major
zones of the respiratory system?

   A) left bronchus and right bronchus

   B) nose and mouth

   C) larynx and pharynx

   D) conducting and respiratory

49. Which of the following is not one of the
major tissue layers of the alimentary canal?

   A) submucosa

   B) muscularis

   C) adventitia

   D) duodenum

50. Which of the following distinguishes the
isotopes of an element?

   A) Isotopes are atoms of the same element
   that have different ionic charges.

   B) Isotopes are atoms of elements within
   the same group on the periodic table.

   C) Isotopes are atoms of the same
   element that have different numbers of
   neutrons.

   D) Isotopes are atoms of the same element
   with different electron configurations.

51. Which of the following is the cartilaginous
flap that protects the larynx from water or
food while still allowing the flow of air?

   A) epiglottis

   B) bronchioles

   C) epithelium

   D) tongue

52. Which of the following describes the
function of the fascia in muscle tissue?

   A) to enclose, protect, support, and
   separate muscle tissue

   B) to connect muscle tissue to bone

   C) to serve as the contractile unit of muscle

   D) to slide past the actin protein cells in
   muscle to create contraction

53. Which of the following correctly describes a strong acid?

   A) A strong acid completely ionizes in water.

   B) A strong acid donates more than one proton.

   C) A strong acid contains at least one metal atom.

   D) A strong acid will not decompose.

54. The process by which blood circulates oxygen from the lungs to the body's tissues is an example of which of the following?

   A) external respiration

   B) internal respiration

   C) inhalation

   D) exhalation

55. Which of the following is the material that is secreted into hair follicles to waterproof and lubricate the skin?

   A) sweat

   B) sebum

   C) vernix caseosa

   D) mucus

56. Which of the following are the connective tissues that attach bone to bone and help strengthen joints?

   A) tendons

   B) cartilage

   C) collagen

   D) ligaments

57. Which of the following is NOT a nucleobase of DNA?

   A) adenine

   B) guanine

   C) thymine

   D) uracil

58. Which of the following materials is the primary structural protein of the epidermis, nails, and skin?

   A) eponychium

   B) collagen

   C) keratin

   D) fibroblast

59. Which of the following correctly describes atomic number?

   A) The atomic number is the number of atoms in a mole of a given substance.

   B) The atomic number is the number of neutrons in an atom.

   C) The atomic number is the number of atoms in a gram of a given substance.

   D) The atomic number is the number of protons in an atom.

60. Which of the following is a descriptive, generalized body of scientific observations?

   A) law

   B) theory

   C) model

   D) hypothesis

61. Which of the following types of cells are the main transporters of oxygen through the body?

   A) goblet cells

   B) white blood cells

   C) red blood cells

   D) platelets

62. Which of the following is the general term for a chemical substance that the body produces and transports through the blood to stimulate a cellular response?

   A) hypophysis

   B) amino acids

   C) oxytocin

   D) hormones

63. Which of the following is NOT a function of hair?

   A) regulation of body temperature

   B) extension of the sensory system

   C) protection from UV radiation

   D) protecting soft tissue from injury

64. Which of the following is NOT one of the functions of proteins found in the phospholipid bilayer of a cell membrane?

   A) to break down material that enters through the cell membrane

   B) to act as receptors that recognize and transmit hormonal messages

   C) to provide an attachment point for other cells

   D) to transport material across the membrane into the cell

65. Which of the following is the muscular action that moves a part of the body away from its median plane?

   A) abduction

   B) adduction

   C) pronation

   D) supination

66. Which of the following does NOT distinguish quantitative data collection from qualitative data collection methods?

   A) Qualitative methods are more open-ended than quantitative.

   B) Results from randomized quantitative methods can be applied to a general population; results from qualitative cannot.

   C) Quantitative methods are number based; qualitative methods are text based.

   D) Qualitative methods do not need to be as valid or reliable as quantitative methods.

67. Which of the following is an example of a birthmark caused by an increased volume of capillaries close to the surface of the skin?

   A) ephelides

   B) vascular nevis

   C) melanocytes

   D) comedones

68. Which of the following correctly describes the valence shell of an atom?

   A) The valence shell is the outermost-occupied electron orbital energy level.

   B) The valence shell is always partially filled with electrons.

   C) The valence shell is found only in ions, not in neutral atoms.

   D) The valence shell must contain p-orbitals.

69. Which of the following describes how skeletal muscles and bones work together to stimulate movement?

   A) Muscles contract and exert force on the bone, which acts as a lever to stimulate movement.

   B) Bones contract and exert force on the muscle, which acts as a lever to stimulate movement.

   C) Muscles elongate, moving the bone involuntarily.

   D) Bones elongate, moving the muscle involuntarily.

70. Which of the following describes the correct order of stages of the cell cycle?

   A) interphase → mitosis → cytokinesis

   B) prophase → metaphase → anaphase → telophase

   C) interphase → meiosis I → meiosis II

   D) gap I → synthesis → gap II

71. Which of the following occurs due to a hypersensitivity in the immune system that causes a major inflammatory response to a common material?

   A) development of antibodies

   B) autoimmune disorders

   C) allergies

   D) AIDS

72. Which of the following is one of the primary muscles that drives ventilation?

   A) thoracic cavity

   B) oblique

   C) lungs

   D) diaphragm

73. White blood cells develop from stem cells located in which of the following organs?

   A) thymus

   B) bone marrow

   C) lymph node

   D) spleen

74. Which of the following describes a gene in which one allele takes a different form from another?

   A) phenotype

   B) heterozygous

   C) homolog

   D) homozygous

75. Which of the following molecules have London dispersion forces?

   A) All atoms and molecules have London dispersion forces.

   B) Atoms and molecules with full valence shells have London dispersion forces.

   C) Atoms and molecules with a noble gas electron configuration have London dispersion forces.

   D) Atoms and molecules that contain at least one metal atom have London dispersion forces.

76. Which of the following are the two proteins found in muscle tissue that cause muscle contraction as they slide past one another?

   A) actin and sarcomeres

   B) actin and myosin

   C) myosin and tropomyosin

   D) troponin and sarcomeres

77. Which of the following is NOT a hormone-producing gland of the endocrine system?

   A) steroid

   B) pituitary

   C) adrenal

   D) thyroid

78. Which of the following is the process in which pathogens are "eaten," or absorbed and digested, by white blood cells as part of an immune response?

   A) pinocytosis

   B) phagocytosis

   C) opsonization

   D) vasodilation

79. Which of the following describes the relationship between correlation and causation?

   A) Correlation implies causation.

   B) Only negative correlation implies causation.

   C) Correlation and causation are mutually exclusive; if one happens, the other cannot.

   D) Correlation does not imply causation.

80. The exchange of gases and blood happens in which of the following parts of the respiratory zone?

   A) alveoli

   B) alveolar duct

   C) pleura

   D) bronchioles

81. Which of the following glands provides nourishment for sperm, as well as the majority of the fluid that combines with sperm to form semen?

   A) seminal vesicles

   B) prostate gland

   C) bulbourethral glands

   D) Cowper's glands

82. Which of the following is the largest branch of the abdominal aorta, which supplies oxygenated blood to the upper digestive tract?

   A) inferior mesenteric artery

   B) gastric artery

   C) celiac artery

   D) superior mesenteric artery

83. Which of the following is NOT a phase of spermatogenesis, or the final stage of sperm formation?

   A) tail formation

   B) cap phase

   C) Golgi phase

   D) fertilization

84. Blood is metabolized in the liver as it passes through which of the following types of blood vessels?

   A) hepatic vein

   B) inferior vena cava

   C) arterioles

   D) sinusoidal capillaries

85. Which of the following is a heterogeneous mixture?

   A) a mixture in which the atoms or molecules are distributed unevenly

   B) a mixture of more than one type of atom or molecule

   C) a mixture of covalent and ionic compounds

   D) a mixture of polar and nonpolar molecules

86. Hormones can be classified into one of four basic groups based on their chemical source. Which of the following groups is derived from cholesterol?

   A) catecholamines

   B) steroids

   C) polypeptides

   D) eicosanoids

87. Which of the following is a definition of adaptation, in the context of evolution?

   A) the process of descent with modification

   B) the increased likelihood that a particular genotype will increase in frequency in a population

   C) the process of individuals in a population choosing mates due to superior characteristics

   D) a biological feature or behavior in a population of organisms that improves its chances for survival in the environment

88. Which of the following is the element of blood that comprises most of its total volume?

   A) plasma

   B) red blood cells

   C) white blood cells

   D) water

89. Which of the following is NOT true for enzyme-catalyzed reactions?

   A) The reaction will speed up if the concentration of substrate increases.

   B) The reaction will speed up if the concentration of enzyme increases.

   C) The reaction will slow down at very low temperatures.

   D) The reaction will speed up without limit as the temperature increases.

90. Which of the following is the molecule found in red blood cells that binds to up to four oxygen molecules?

A) hemoglobin

B) erythrocytes

C) globulin

D) antigens

91. Which of the following is NOT a reason why randomization is critical in experimental design, especially in experiments with human subjects?

A) to give humans no choice but to participate

B) to eliminate selection bias

C) to provide a statistical basis

D) to provide a balanced group of subjects

92. Which of the following is the division of the nervous system primarily responsible for regulating all involuntary and subconscious muscle functions?

A) somatic nervous system

B) autonomic nervous system

C) sympathetic nervous system

D) peripheral nervous system

93. Which of the following is an appendage of a neuron that sends electrical signals away from the neuron cell?

A) axon

B) dendrite

C) neurite

D) neuroglia

94. Which of the following is the definition of action potential in a neuron?

A) a connection between two neurons

B) an electrical impulse that is transported down a neuron in response to a stimulus

C) an imbalanced electrical charge that exists in an inactive nerve cell

D) a chemical signal between two nerve cells

95. Which of the following are the three major portions of the brain?

A) cerebellum, spinal cord, white matter

B) cerebrum, temporal lobe, occipital lobe

C) pons, medulla oblongata, brain stem

D) cerebrum, cerebellum, brain stem

96. Which of the following describes how a catalyst speeds up a reaction?

A) A catalyst participates in the reaction, making it go faster.

B) A catalyst speeds up a reaction by causing lower energy products to be made.

C) A catalyst lowers the activation energy by providing an alternate route for the reaction.

D) A catalyst causes the reactants to collide more frequently.

97. Which of the following is the final vessel through which semen must pass before being expelled from the body?

A) ejaculatory duct

B) penile urethra

C) membranous urethra

D) vas deferens

98. Which of the following groups of bones are part of the axial skeleton?

A) pectoral girdle

B) rib cage

C) arms and hands

D) pelvic girdle

99. Which of the following types of variables is changed in a scientific experiment?

A) controlled variable

B) measured variable

C) dependent variable

D) independent variable

100. The vertebral column consists of thirty-three vertebrae and is divided into several groups. Which of the following describes the lumbar vertebrae?

A) seven vertebrae located in the neck that connect the vertebral column to the skull, allowing for neck rotation

B) five vertebrae that are fused in the pelvis, forming a supportive, wedge-shaped bone

C) twelve vertebrae located in the upper back, each of which connects to the base of a rib

D) five vertebrae located in the lower back, which support most of the body's weight

101. Which type of hypothesis assumes no relationship between two variables?

A) scientific hypothesis

B) working hypothesis

C) null hypothesis

D) alternate hypothesis

102. Which of the following describes the applicability of a research conclusion to situations outside the experiment?

A) internal validity

B) test validity

C) external validity

D) content validity

103. Which of the following is NOT one of the three types of muscles found in the human body?

A) skeletal

B) cardiac

C) soft

D) smooth

104. Which of the following is the structure of the male reproductive system that stores spermatozoa during the maturation process?

A) vas deferens

B) scrotum

C) epididymis

D) testicular artery

105. Which of the following types of hormones stimulates a chemical response to a target cell by diffusing through the cell membrane to bind to the receptors inside the cell?

A) fat-soluble hormones

B) amino acid derivatives

C) hydrophilic hormones

D) water-soluble hormones

106. Which of the following is an example of human error in an experiment?

A) an imperfectly calibrated scale

B) contaminating a sterile sample by breathing on it

C) a draft in the laboratory slightly changing the temperature of a liquid

D) failure to account for wind speed when measuring distance traveled

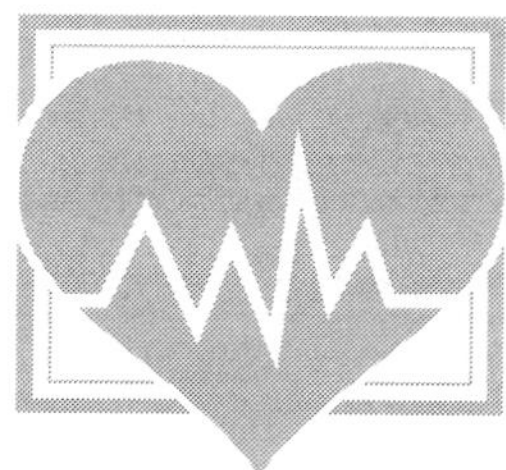

ANSWER KEY

1. **B) is correct.** Oxygen intake and carbon dioxide disposal are the primary functions of the respiratory system.

2. **B) is correct.** Making observations is the first step of the scientific method; observations enable the researcher to form a question and begin the research process.

3. **D) is correct.** The mechanism of natural selection is rooted in the idea that there is variation in inherited traits among a population of organisms, and that there is differential reproduction as a result.

4. **A) is correct.** Gonadotrophs produce both FSH and LH, which play a key role in ovulation, lactation, sperm development, and testosterone production.

5. **B) is correct.** Ovarian follicles each contain a sac with an immature egg, or oocyte. During the female reproductive cycle, several oocytes will mature into a mature ovum. Eventually, one ovum is released per cycle during ovulation.

6. **B) is correct.** The tongue is a muscle that plays a primary role in digestion and, in conjunction with teeth, prepares food for swallowing.

7. **A) is correct.** The left atrium receives oxygenated blood, then moves it downward into the left ventricle.

8. **C) is correct.** The parietal lobe is considered the primary sensory processing and integrating center of the brain.

9. **C) is correct.** The humoral immune response is characterized by the mediation and production of antibodies. In this adaptive response, B lymphocytes recognize and attach pathogens together to prevent dispersal.

10. **A) is correct.** Data is considered reliable if similar results are found after repeated experiments following consistent conditions; however, if data does not accurately measure the variable it is intended to measure, it is not considered valid.

11. **C) is correct.** Mendel's law of independent assortment, his second law of heredity, expands on the law of segregation by stipulating that alleles which separate in the gamete stage do so independently of other genes.

12. **B) is correct.** Proceeding top to bottom on the periodic table, atoms gain more and more layers of electrons in their

orbitals, increasing radius. Proceeding right to left on the periodic table, atoms have fewer valence electrons and the attraction between nucleus and electrons decreases. Both of these effects cause a trend of increasing radius down and to the left on the periodic table.

13. **C) is correct.** Enamel is a tissue found in teeth, but not skeletal bones.

14. **B) is correct.** Semilunar valves are present in the pulmonary trunk and the aortic trunk; they allow blood to enter the vessels and prevent its return back to the heart.

15. **A) is correct.** Calcium is the most abundant mineral found in bones, as well as the entire body.

16. **C) is correct.** The skin, which provides a seamless layer of cells around the entire body, is the primary physical barrier that prevents pathogens from entering the body.

17. **D) is correct.** Neuromuscular junctions are the location in which the nervous system communicates with the muscular system to create muscle contraction and movement.

18. **B) is correct.** The medulla oblongata, along with the pons, is a portion of the brain stem that regulates critical body functions.

19. **A) is correct.** The pyloric sphincter acts as a valve at the connection of the stomach and small intestine.

20. **B) is correct.** A released ovum stays in the fallopian tube for approximately 24 hours. If sperm have not migrated up the tubes to fertilize the egg, then it moves through the uterus; if fertilization does occur, it stays in the tube for several more days as it moves to the uterus for implantation.

21. **C) is correct.** The pineal gland is located in the epithalamus and is a gland involved in the production of melatonin.

22. **B) is correct.** Inferential statistics are used to analyze and apply data beyond the immediate data from an observation or experiment.

23. **C) is correct.** Lipids, which include but are not limited to fats, are an efficient source of energy storage due to their ability to store nearly twice as much energy as carbohydrates and proteins.

24. **B) is correct.** The sinoatrial (SA) node is an area of specialized muscle tissue in the right atrium that generates an electrical signal which spreads from cell to cell to generate the heartbeat.

25. **A) is correct.** Ganglions are dense clusters of nerve cells responsible for processing sensory information and coordinating motor activity.

26. **A) is correct.** Surface absorptive cells (SAC) line the intestinal microvilli to absorb food material as it passes through the intestine.

27. **C) is correct.** Ossification is the general term referring to the formation or conversion of bone by osteoblasts.

28. **A) is correct.** Cytokines are small proteins released by cells and have a great impact on cell communication and behavior. There are many kinds of cytokines with a great variety of functions; in the immune system, some cytokines play a critical role in immune response activation by triggering inflammation, fever, and other responses.

29. **A) is correct.** This is the path air follows through the respiratory system during gas exchange.

30. **A) is correct.** Expression of secondary sexual characteristics is regulated by estrogen.

31.   **C) is correct.** The hypodermis is the thickest layer of skin and is the site of much of the stored fat in the human body.

32.   **C) is correct.** Synapses are connections between two neurons. Nerve signals trigger the release of neurotransmitters, which carry the nerve impulse across the synaptic cleft, or gap, between cells, to be received by the receptor site of the next cell.

33.   **D) is correct.** Hund's rule states that electrons fill orbitals in a specific order, and they fill orbitals singly with similar spin before pairing.

34.   **C) is correct.** The large intestine, or colon, is an s-shaped organ that dehydrates food material as it travels through the organ and is eliminated at the rectum.

35.   **B) is correct.** Using one filtration system for all three tanks keeps the water quality across all three tanks constant and eliminates experimental bias for this variable.

36.   **C) is correct.** A controlled experiment requires researchers to compare an experimental group with a control group while controlling all variables except for the independent variable, which the researcher manipulates to test the hypothesis.

37.   **A) is correct.** Tank A is the control group because the sunlight variable is unchanged from the sunlight the elodea are exposed to in their natural environment.

38.   **D) is correct.** T cells are a type of white blood cell that originates in the thymus. There are four different varieties of mature T cells, each of which serves a different function in the immune system.

39.   **D) is correct.** Veins are blood vessels that move blood to the heart using a series of valves.

40.   **A) is correct.** The smooth endoplasmic reticulum is a series of membranes attached to the cell nucleus and plays an important role in the production and storage of lipids. It is called smooth because it lacks ribosomes on the membrane surface.

41.   **B) is correct.** Precision describes measurements that are consistently close to one another and the average measurement.

42.   **B) is correct.** The sister chromatids of each chromosome are pulled apart by the spindle and pulled to opposite centrosomes during anaphase, elongating the cell in the process.

43.   **D) is correct.** Peristalsis begins in the esophagus, where the bolus of food material is swallowed, and continues to transport food to the stomach, the small intestine, and the large intestine.

44.   **D) is correct.** Insulin production and blood sugar regulation are performed by the pancreas.

45.   **D) is correct.** Combustion is defined as a reaction with O_2 in order to produce CO_2 and H_2O.

46.   **A) is correct.** Both the pancreas and salivary glands produce amylase, which is an enzyme that helps digest carbohydrates.

47.   **A) is correct.** A hypertonic solution has a higher concentration than the interior of the cell, and water will rush out of the cell to equalize the concentrations, causing the cell to shrink.

48.   **D) is correct.** The conducting zone consists of the upper respiratory tract from the nose and mouth through the trachea; it filters and conducts air into the lungs. The respiratory zone consists of the lower respiratory tract from the

bronchioles to the alveoli and serves as a site of gas exchange.

49. **D) is correct.** The duodenum is a region of the small intestine that neutralizes materials entering from the stomach.

50. **C) is correct.** Isotopes are atoms that differ in their number of neutrons but are otherwise identical.

51. **A) is correct.** The epiglottis is the protective flap at the entrance of the larynx.

52. **A) is correct.** Fascia is connective tissue that encloses individual muscle fibers.

53. **A) is correct.** Strong acids break apart into their constituent ions immediately when placed in water.

54. **B) is correct.** Internal respiration is the process that occurs after oxygen leaves the lungs via the alveoli.

55. **B) is correct.** Sebum is secreted by the sebaceous glands in order to coat and prevent hair and skin from drying.

56. **D) is correct.** Ligaments are made of flexible collagen fibers and play a key role in joint movement and bone stabilization.

57. **D) is correct.** Uracil (U) is a pyrimidine found in RNA, replacing the thymine (T) pyrimidine found in DNA.

58. **C) is correct.** Keratin, produced by keratinocytes, makes up the majority of the epidermis structure, hair, and nails.

59. **D) is correct.** The atomic number is the number of protons in an atom and defines the type of atom. Elements are arranged on the periodic table in order of increasing atomic number.

60. **A) is correct.** Scientific laws, like Newton's laws of gravity or Mendel's laws of heredity, describe phenomena in the natural world that have repeatedly occurred with no known exceptions yet.

61. **C) is correct.** Red blood cells contain hemoglobin, which is a molecule that transports oxygen.

62. **D) is correct.** Hormones are considered chemical mediators of the endocrine system and depend on the circulatory system for distribution. They elicit responses by binding to cellular receptors at the targeted tissues.

63. **D) is correct.** Nails, not hair, help protect soft tissue from injury.

64. **A) is correct.** Cytoplasm breaks down material that enters through the cell membrane.

65. **A) is correct.** Abduction occurs when muscles contract and move a body part away from the midline; the muscle completing this movement is called an abductor muscle.

66. **D) is correct.** Both qualitative and quantitative methods must be held to the same standard of scientific rigor.

67. **B) is correct.** A vascular nevis, or hemangioma, is a red-colored birthmark caused by a proliferation of blood vessels.

68. **A) is correct.** The valence shell is the electron orbital shell that is furthest from the nucleus and incompletely filled.

69. **A) is correct.** Muscles contract and exert force on the bone, working in tandem to create movement.

70. **A) is correct.** The cell cycle consists of three stages: interphase, or cell growth; mitosis, the division of chromosomes and nucleus; and cytokinesis, the division of the cytoplasm.

71. **C) is correct.** Allergies occur when the immune system treats a common foreign substance as a pathogen and attacks the substance with the IgE antibody.

72.   **D) is correct.** The diaphragm is a muscle that increases the thoracic cavity when contracted, allowing more space for the lungs during respiration.

73.   **B) is correct.** All white blood cells begin to develop in bone marrow; some of these cells mature in the bone marrow and are called B cells.

74.   **B) is correct.** A heterozygous gene contains two alleles that are different from one another; one will be expressed as the dominant allele in the phenotype.

75.   **A) is correct.** London dispersion forces arise due to the random movement of electrons and may be found in all atoms and molecules.

76.   **B) is correct.** As actin and myosin molecules in muscle bands slide past one another, they pull the opposite ends of the cell toward one another and create contraction by shortening the length of the muscle.

77.   **A) is correct.** Steroids are a type of cholesterol-derived hormone.

78.   **B) is correct.** Phagocytosis is an important innate immune response to pathogens, in which foreign bodies are ingested and destroyed by phagocytic cells.

79.   **D) is correct.** Correlation is a measure of the relationship between two variables; causation only exists if one variable (cause) impacts the other (effect).

80.   **A) is correct.** Alveoli are sacs at the end of the respiratory tree in the lungs and are the area of gas exchange.

81.   **A) is correct.** The seminal vesicles provide nourishment for sperm and up to 70 percent of the total volume of semen.

82.   **C) is correct.** The celiac artery is the first and largest branch of the abdominal aorta and supplies oxygenated blood to the stomach, spleen, liver, and esophagus.

83.   **D) is correct.** Fertilization does not occur until after sperm has fully matured and been released to an egg.

84.   **D) is correct.** Blood is metabolized by liver cells in the sinusoidal capillaries before exiting the liver via the hepatic vein.

85.   **A) is correct.** A heterogeneous mixture is any non-uniform mixture, which means that the atoms or molecules are unevenly distributed.

86.   **B) is correct.** Steroid hormones, such as testosterone, are lipid-soluble hormones derived from cholesterol.

87.   **D) is correct.** Adaptations are features that are taken on by a population—the result of the process of evolution.

88.   **A) is correct.** Plasma, the liquid portion of blood, comprises more than half of total blood volume in the average adult.

89.   **D) is correct.** This statement is false; at a very high temperature, the enzyme will become denatured and will no longer be capable of catalyzing the reaction.

90.   **A) is correct.** Hemoglobin in red blood cells binds to oxygen molecules and transports them from the lungs throughout the body.

91.   **A) is correct.** All experiments involving humans must use only willing volunteers; scientists must never coerce unwilling subjects. This ethical consideration is unrelated to randomization.

92.   **B) is correct.** The autonomic nervous system regulates involuntary functions of the heart, digestive tract, and other smooth muscles; it is further subdivided into the sympathetic and parasympathetic nervous systems.

93. **A) is correct.** Neurons typically have one long, thick axon that transmits signals away from the neuron.

94. **B) is correct.** An action potential is the quick rise and fall of the electrical potential in a neuron.

95. **D) is correct.** The cerebrum, cerebellum, and brain stem are considered the three major portions of the brain; all brain regions are found within these three portions.

96. **C) is correct.** A catalyst makes it possible for a reaction to proceed by an alternative route, thus lowering the activation energy and speeding up the reaction.

97. **B) is correct.** Both urine and semen travel through the penile urethra, the longest portion of the male urethra, to be expelled through the urethral opening.

98. **B) is correct.** The rib cage, which consists of the ribs and the sternum, is part of the axial skeleton.

99. **D) is correct.** The independent variable is changed by the researcher during an experiment; this change may or may not cause a direct change in the dependent variable.

100. **D) is correct.** The five lumbar vertebrae are found in the lower back where the spine curves down toward the abdomen.

101. **C) is correct.** A null hypothesis assumes that any relationship is due to chance.

102. **C) is correct.** External validity can be further divided into two types: population validity, a measure of how applicable conclusions are to a population, and ecological validity, a measure of how much the situation impacts the experiment results.

103. **C) is correct.** All muscle tissues are considered soft tissue; therefore, soft muscle is not considered a separate type of muscle in the human body.

104. **C) is correct.** The epididymis is a coiled tube that receives spermatozoa and stores them for up to three months before transporting them to the vas deferens.

105. **A) is correct.** Fat-soluble, or lipophilic, hormones pass through cell membranes to attach to receptors. The receptors then bind to DNA to activate the targeted gene.

106. **B) is correct.** This is an example of human error, or error that occurs when the researcher makes a mistake.

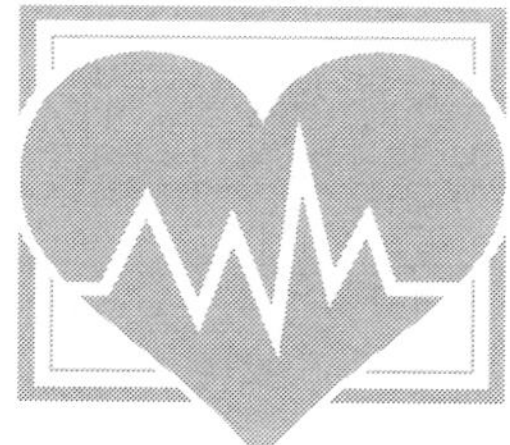

VOCABULARY AND GRAMMAR

Directions: Read the question carefully, and choose the best answer.

1. Which of the following sentences follows the rules of capitalization?

   A) As juveniles, african white-backed vultures are darkly colored, developing their white feathers only as they grow into adulthood.

   B) Ukrainians celebrate a holiday called *Malanka* during which men dress in costumes and masks and play tricks on their neighbors.

   C) Because of its distance from the sun, the planet neptune has seasons that last the equivalent of forty-one earth years.

   D) Edward Jenner, considered the Father of immunology, invented the world's first vaccine.

2. Sandra's principal reason for choosing the job was that it would be full-time and would offer benefits.

   Which of the following is the complete subject in the sentence?

   A) Sandra's principal reason for choosing the job

   B) Sandra's principal reason

   C) Sandra's principal

   D) Sandra

3. James had already been awake for nineteen hours____ after a twelve-hour work day, when he received the news.

   A) .

   B) ;

   C) ,

   D) —

4. First and foremost, they receive an <u>annual pension payment. The amount of the pension</u> has been reviewed and changed a number of times, most recently to reflect the salary of a high-level government executive.

   Which of the following would NOT be an acceptable way to revise and combine the underlined portion of the sentences above?

   A) annual pension payment, the amount of which

   B) annual pension payment; the amount of the pension

   C) annual pension payment; over the years since 1958, the amount of the pension

   D) annual pension payment, the amount of the pension

5. Which of the following sentences has the correct subject-verb agreement?

   A) The Akhal-Teke horse breed, originally from Turkmenistan, have long enjoyed a reputation for bravery and fortitude.

   B) The employer decided that he could not, due to the high cost of healthcare, afford to offer other benefits to his employees.

   C) Though Puerto Rico is known popularly for its beaches, its landscape also include mountains, which play home to many of the island's rural villages.

   D) Each of the storm chasers decide whether or not to go out when rain makes visibility low.

6. Which of the following is a compound sentence?

   A) Plague, generally not a major public health concern, actually continues to spread among rodent populations today, and it even occasionally makes its way into a human host.

   B) Modern archeology, which seeks answers to humanity's questions about its past, is helped significantly by new technologies.

   C) In the fight against obesity, countries around the world are imposing taxes on sodas and other sugary drinks in an effort to curb unhealthy habits.

   D) Because the assassination of President John F. Kennedy continues to haunt and fascinate Americans, new movies, books, and television series about it are being released every year.

7. Parrots, among the most intelligent birds in the world, have been prized pets for many centuries; in fact, the first recorded instance of parrot training was written in the thirteenth century.

   Which of the following is a synonym for *prized* as used in the sentence?

   A) unlikely

   B) misunderstood

   C) rewarded

   D) valued

8. Which of the following would most likely be found in an academic research paper on the world's food supply?

   A) It's ridiculous that so many people in the world are hungry while others just throw away tons of uneaten food.

   B) I've always believed that it's our moral duty as a people to provide food and clean water to those who do not have access to it, which is why I have made research of the food supply my life's work.

   C) Advances in agricultural technology over the past five decades have led to a steady increase in the global food supply, and the populations of many countries around the world are benefitting.

   D) Poor people should appeal to their governments for help feeding their families.

9. Which of the following prefixes would be used to indicate that something is *inside* or *within*?

   A) intra–

   B) trans–

   C) anti–

   D) hyper–

10. Which of the following is correctly punctuated?

   A) The artist Prince, whose death shocked America in April of 2016; was one of the most successful musical artists of the last century.

   B) The artist Prince, whose death shocked America in April of 2016, was one of the most successful musical artists of the last century.

   C) The artist Prince—whose death shocked America in April of 2016, was one of the most successful musical artists of the last century.

   D) The artist Prince, whose death shocked America in April of 2016: was one of the most successful musical artists of the last century.

11. Everyday items like potatos, bread, onions, and even saliva are the tools of art conservators, who work to clean and restore works of art.

Which of the following is misspelled in the sentence above?

A) potatos

B) saliva

C) conservators

D) restore

12. Today, astrophysicists study the same stars that were observed by the astronemers of the ancient world, though today's techniques and technology are much more advanced.

Which of the following is misspelled in the sentence?

A) astrophysicists

B) astronemers

C) techniques

D) technology

13. Which of the following nouns is written in the correct plural form?

A) vertebraes

B) gooses

C) octopusses

D) bronchi

14. Which of the following sentences is irrelevant as part of a paragraph composed of these sentences?

A) Traffic around the arena was heavy, so we were worried we'd miss the opening pitch.

B) My brother and I won tickets in a radio station contest to see his favorite team play on opening day.

C) To win the contest, you had to be the 395th caller and know the answer to a trivia question; we waited anxiously by the phone for the contest to begin.

D) My brother has followed the team since childhood, so we knew he'd be able to answer the trivia question correctly.

15. The American Academy of Arts and Sciences includes members whose topics of study span many disciplines such as math, science, arts, humanities, public affairs, and business.

Which of the following is an appropriate synonym for *disciplines* as it is used in the sentence?

A) locations

B) regions

C) punishments

D) fields

16. Which of the following is a complex sentence?

A) When skywriting, a pilot flies a small aircraft in specific, particular formations, creating large letters visible from the ground.

B) The public defense attorney was able to maintain her optimism despite her dearth of courtroom wins, her lack of free time, and her growing list of clients.

C) Because the distance between stars in the galaxy is far greater than the distance between planets, interstellar travel is expected to be an even bigger challenge than interplanetary exploration.

D) Invented in France in the early nineteenth century, the stethoscope underwent a number of reiterations before the emergence of the modern form of the instrument in the 1850s.

17. Unlike a traditional comic book, a graphic novel is released as one single publication, either in the form of one long story or in the form of an anthology.

Which of the following is an appropriate synonym for *traditional* as it is used in the sentence?

A) old-fashioned

B) conventional

C) expensive

D) popular

18. Which of the following statements is true regarding the outline?

1. Types of Engines

A.   Heat engines
        i)   Combustion engines
        ii)   Non-combustion heat engines

B.   Electric engines

C.   Physically powered motors
        i)   Pneumatic motors
        ii)   Hydraulic motors

A) Heat engines are the most common type of engine.

B) Pneumatic and hydraulic motors are both types of electric engines.

C) The three types of engines are heat engines, electric engines, and pneumatic motors.

D) Heat engines can be broken down into combustion and non-combustion engines.

19. The patient's preoperative evaluation is scheduled for next Wednesday.

In the sentence, the prefix *pre–* indicates that the evaluation will take place at which of the following times?

A) before the operation

B) after the operation

C) during the operation

D) at the end of the operation

20. Which of the following root words would be used in a word related to the body?

A) corp

B) auto

C) man

D) bio

21. Her new tennis racket cost her a hundred bucks, but it was worth the steep price tag.

Which of the following words from the sentence is slang?

A) cost

B) bucks

C) steep

D) tag

22. Though professional dental care is widely available in the developed world, the prevalence of cavities is much higher there.

Which of the following parts of speech is *widely* as used in the sentence?

A) adjective

B) noun

C) adverb

D) verb

23. Typically, water that has evaporated remains in the sky in cloud form for less than ten days before falling to Earth again as precipitation.

Which of the following parts of speech is *remains* as used in the sentence?

A) noun

B) verb

C) adjective

D) adverb

24. Though the term *nomad* is often associated with early populations, nomadic cultures exist today, especially in the mountain's of Europe and Asia.

Which of the following punctuation marks is used incorrectly?

A) the comma after *populations*

B) the comma after *today*

C) the apostrophe in *mountain's*

D) the period after *Asia*

25. On Parents' Day, a public holiday in the Democratic Republic of Congo, families celebrate parents' both living and deceased.

Which of the following punctuation marks is used incorrectly?

A) the apostrophe in *Parents' Day*

B) the comma following *Day*

C) the comma following *Congo*

D) the apostrophe in *parents'*

26. Unfortunately, the belief that changelings could be convinced to leave was not just <u>an innocuous superstition. On some occasions,</u> harm came to the individual who was thought to be a changeling.

Which is the best way to revise and combine the underlined portion of the sentences?

A) an innocuous superstition, on some occasions,

B) an innocuous superstition, but on some occasions,

C) an innocuous superstition; however, on some occasions,

D) an innocuous superstition: on some occasions,

27. Which of the following phrases follows the rules of capitalization?

A) President Carter and his advisors

B) Robert Jones, the senior Senator from California

C) my Aunt and Uncle who live out west

D) the party on New Year's eve

28. In 1983, almost twenty years after his death, T.S. Eliot won two Tony Awards for his contributions to the well-loved musical *Cats*.

Cats is italicized for which of the following reasons?

A) to highlight its importance

B) to indicate it is intentionally misspelled

C) because it is the title of a musical

D) because it is in a foreign language

29. Which of the following sentences has correct pronoun-antecedent agreement?

A) The storm, which included three days of rain, was very strong, and they left half the city flooded.

B) Each of the cars needs to be examined for damage by a mechanic; he may need repairs.

C) The number of people who had to evacuate hasn't been confirmed, but it is small.

D) Many people were able to take advantage of shelters, where he or she was kept safe from the storm.

30. The *Chicago Tribune* is famous for many reasons: in 1948, the paper published an erroneous headline about the winner of the Presidential election, and in 1974, it called for President Nixon's resignation.

Which of the following phrases contains an error in capitalization?

A) *Chicago Tribune*

B) the paper

C) Presidential election

D) President Nixon's

31. In the eighteenth century, renowned composer Wolfgang Amadeus Mozart set to music the poetry of a famous, well–known writer who shared his name–Johann Wolfgang von Goethe.

Which of the following punctuation marks correctly completes the sentence?

A) ,

B) :

C) ;

D) ?

→
CONTINUE

32. Which of the following sentences has the correct subject-verb agreement?

A) The Iris and B. Gerald Cantor Roof Garden, atop the Metropolitan Museum of Art in New York City, offer a remarkable view.

B) The Mammoth-Flint Ridge Cave System, located in central Kentucky inside Mammoth Cave National Park, are the largest cave system in the world.

C) Andy Warhol's paintings, in addition to being the subject of the largest single-artist museum in the United States, are in great demand.

D) The field of child development are concerned with the emotional, psychological, and biological developments of infants and children.

33. Which of the following would most likely be found in a scientific paper on the history of telescopes?

A) Jerry R. Ehman had always encouraged his kids' love of science by taking them camping and star gazing.

B) In 1977, Jerry R. Ehman, using a powerful radio telescope, detected a signal that seemed to come from outside the Earth's atmosphere.

C) I believe that telescopes have the potential to change our understanding of the universe and our place in it.

D) It's really silly to think that telescopes are a new invention.

34. Vivariums, common in elementary school classrooms, are enclosed spaces designed to replicate a particular habitat.

Which of the following is part of the predicate in the sentence?

A) are enclosed spaces

B) vivariums

C) elementary school classrooms

D) common in

35. The Boat Race, a rowing race that has been held almost annually in London, England, since 1856, was infamously interupted in 2012.

Which of the following is misspelled in the sentence?

A) rowing

B) annually

C) infamously

D) interupted

36. The exotic pet trade is a significant concern for enviornmentalists and animal rights advocates around the world.

Which of the following is misspelled in the sentence?

A) significant

B) enviornmentalists

C) rights

D) advocates

37. In baseball today, strict regulations have standardized the design of bats; they used to come in a wide range of shapes, sizes, and weights.

Which of the following is a synonym for *standardized* as used in the sentence?

A) clarified

B) reconciled

C) normalized

D) ignored

38. Which of the following sentences has correct pronoun-antecedent agreement?

A) Animals use estivation to avoid harsh conditions and to help it survive winter.

B) Some species of fish use luminescent lures to trick other fish into moving closer to it.

C) In a parasitic relationship, one species is negatively affected while the other species acquires what they need to survive.

D) Tropical rainforests are made up of many layers, each of which has its own distinct species.

39. Which of the following prefixes would be used to indicate that something is opposite?

A) fore–

B) bi–

C) anti–

D) trans–

40. Which of the following is an appropriate synonym for *insolent* as it is used in the sentence?

The students' insolent behavior drove the teacher to punish the class with extra homework.

A) confusing

B) disrespectful

C) delightful

D) unlikely

41. Which of the following root words would be used in a word related to time?

A) gram

B) crypt

C) chron

D) mort

42. Which of the following is correctly punctuated?

A) In addition to the disastrous effects an active volcano can have on it's immediate surroundings, an eruption can also pose a threat to passing aircraft.

B) In addition to the disastrous effects an active volcano can have on it's immediate surroundings: an eruption can also pose a threat to passing aircraft.

C) In addition to the disastrous effects an active volcano can have on its immediate surroundings: an eruption can also pose a threat to passing aircraft.

D) In addition to the disastrous effects an active volcano can have on its immediate surroundings, an eruption can also pose a threat to passing aircraft.

43. Which of the following would be an acceptable way to combine the two clauses?

A) While these incidents sometimes end in funny or heartwarming stories, at other times they end in fear and destruction.

B) While these incidents sometimes end in funny or heartwarming stories; at other times they end in fear and destruction.

C) While these incidents sometimes end in funny or heartwarming stories: at other times they end in fear and destruction.

D) While these incidents sometimes end in funny or heartwarming stories— at other times they end in fear and destruction.

44. L.L. Zamenhof, an ophthalmologist in the late 1800s, invented a universal language called Esperanto with the goal of advancing international communications and relations.

Which of the following is an appropriate synonym for *advancing* as it is used in the sentence?

A) improving

B) changing

C) hastening

D) celebrating

45. Which of the following is a simple sentence?

A) Although Sacagawea is famous for her role as guide and interpreter for Lewis and Clark, few know about the mystery surrounding her death.

B) The high death toll at the end of the Civil War was not exclusively due to battle losses; large numbers of soldiers died as a result of poor living conditions.

C) Self-driving vehicles are just now being introduced on the automotive market, but research into automating vehicle processes began as early as the 1920s.

D) Freediving is sometimes combined with other underwater activities such as photography, football, hockey, and even target shooting.

46. The distinguished lexicologist had been with the university for many years.

In the sentence, the prefix *lexi–* indicates that the researcher studies which of the following?

A) literature

B) words

C) plants

D) rocks

47. Which of the following is a complex sentence?

A) Engineers designed seat belts to stop the inertia of traveling bodies by applying an opposing force to the driver and passengers during a collision.

B) Hurricanes cost the United States roughly $5 billion per year in damages and have been the cause of almost two million deaths in the last two hundred years.

C) Woodstock appeared in the *Peanuts* comic strips as early as April of 1967, but he was not named until June of 1970, ten months after the famous music festival of the same name, Woodstock.

D) Although organized firefighting groups existed as early as ancient Egyptian times, the first fully state-run brigade was created by Emperor Augustus of Rome.

48. Which of the following sentences is irrelevant as part of a paragraph composed of these sentences?

A) It looks like the weather might force us to move the game to next weekend.

B) Our team will be playing our biggest rival for the last game of the season.

C) The teams play each other every year, and it's a big event for the town.

D) Last year, the mayor closed down Main Street so fans could celebrate together safely.

49. Which of the following parts of speech is *handsome* as it is used in the sentence?

According to Greek mythology, Narcissus was a hunter who was so handsome that he fell in love with his own reflection.

A) noun

B) verb

C) adjective

D) adverb

50. It's a drag to do homework on the weekend, but I won't pass the class if I spend all day watching TV.

Which of the following words from the sentence is slang?

A) homework

B) pass

C) spend

D) drag

51. In many European countries such as, France, Spain, and Italy, hot chocolate is made with real melted chocolate making for a beverage that is thick and rich.

Which of the following punctuation marks is used incorrectly?

A) the comma after "as"

B) the comma after "France"

C) the comma after "Italy"

D) the period after "rich"

52. Which of the following nouns is written in the correct plural form?

A) shelves

B) phenomenons

C) mans

D) deers

53. Abby's travels in Asia provided her the opportunity to try many foods that she would not have been able to try at home in the United States.

Which of the following parts of speech is *travels* as used in the sentence?

A) verb

B) noun

C) adjective

D) adverb

54. Although the Nile River in Africa, passes through eleven countries, it is the main water source of only two of them—Egypt and Sudan.

Which of the following punctuation marks is used incorrectly?

A) the comma after *Africa*

B) the comma after *countries*

C) the em-dash after *them*

D) the period after *Sudan*

55. Spelunking involves much more than adrenaline: enthusiasts dive into unexplored caves <u>to study structures of, take photographs, and create maps of</u> the untouched systems.

Which is the best way to revise the underlined portion of the sentences?

A) to study structures of, take photographs, and create maps of

B) to study structures of, to take photographs, and create maps of

C) to study structures of, taking photographs of, and creating maps of

D) to study structures, take photographs, and create maps of

56. Which of the following statements is true regarding the outline?

1. The Stages of Labor		
A)	First Stage	
		A) Early Phase
		B) Active Phase
		C) Transition Phase
B)	Second Stage	
		1. Pushing
		2. Fetal Expulsion
C)	Third Stage	
D)	Fourth Stage	

A) The Fourth Stage of labor is broken down into two phases.

B) The First Stage of labor is the longest.

C) The First Stage of labor is broken into three phases.

D) Pushing and Fetal Expulsion are parts of the Third Stage of labor.

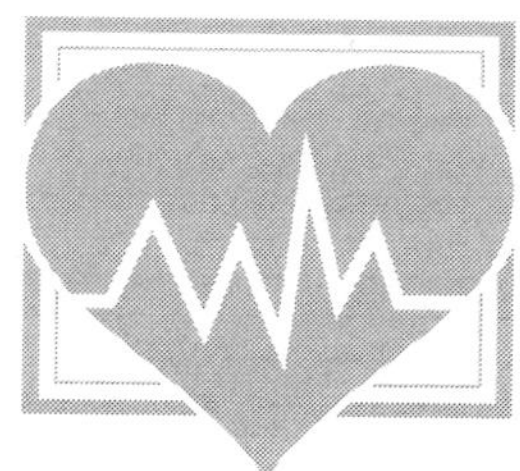

ANSWER KEY

1. **B) is correct.** Both *Ukrainians* and *Malanka* must be capitalized; both are proper nouns, and *Ukrainians* begins a sentence.

2. **A) is correct.** The complete subject includes the main noun (*reason*) and all its accompanying modifying phrases.

3. **C) is correct.** The inessential phrase *after a twelve-hour work day* is being set apart from the rest of the sentence by commas.

4. **D) is correct.** This choice creates a comma splice.

5. **B) is correct.** The verb is the singular *afford*, and its subject is the singular *employer*.

6. **A) is correct.** Here, two independent clauses are connected by a comma plus the coordinating conjunction *and*.

7. **D) is correct.** If these intelligent birds have been kept as pets for so long and if people have taken the time to train them, it is most likely that parrots are *valued* animals.

8. **C) is correct.** This choice uses formal language, the third-person perspective, and non-judgmental language.

9. **A) is correct.** The prefix *intra–* means *inside* or *within*.

10. **B) is correct.** The inessential appositive phrase *whose death shocked America in April of 2016* is correctly set apart from the rest of the sentence by commas. Choices A and D create sentence fragments, and Choice C incorrectly pairs an em dash with a comma.

11. **A) is correct.** *Potatos* should be spelled *potatoes*.

12. **B) is correct.** *Astronemers* should be spelled *astronomers*.

13. **D) is correct.** The noun *bronchus* is made plural by changing the *–us* to *–i*.

14. **A) is correct.** This sentence does not relate to the flow of information provided by the other three, which tell the story of the siblings' experience with the radio contest. It only discusses the siblings' experience attending the game itself.

15. **D) is correct.** *Fields* best describes the idea that members study many different areas of knowledge; furthermore, the word *field* may refer to something intangible. There are many topics of study in many *fields*, or disciplines.

16. **C) is correct.** This sentence includes an independent clause (*interstellar travel is expected to be an even bigger challenge than interplanetary exploration*) and a dependent clause (*Because the distance between stars in the galaxy is far greater than the distance between planets*).

17. **B) is correct.** *Conventional* best describes the idea that comic books have an established narrative framework, a main point in the sentence.

18. **D) is correct.** The two subheadings under "Heat Engines" are "Combustion Engines" and "Non-Combustion Engines."

19. **A) is correct.** The prefix *pre–* means *before*.

20. **A) is correct.** The root word *corp* means *body*.

21. **B) is correct.** *Bucks* is a slang term for *dollars*.

22. **C) is correct.** *Widely* is an adverb modifying the adjective *available*.

23. **B) is correct.** *Remains* is a verb in the sentence.

24. **C) is correct.** *Mountain's* is not possessive in this sentence, so it does not require an apostrophe.

25. **D) is correct.** The second *parents* is plural, not possessive, so it does not require an apostrophe.

26. **D) is correct.** The colon correctly signifies that the second clause builds on the first.

27. **A) is correct.** *President* is a title and should be capitalized when it precedes a name.

29. **C) is correct.** The titles of musicals are always italicized.

28. **C) is correct.** *Number* is singular, so it agrees with the singular pronoun *it*.

30. **C) is correct.** *Presidential* is an adjective describing the election and, as such, should not be capitalized.

31. **B) is correct.** The text following the explanation elaborates on what was said in the first part of the sentence, and is not an independent clause, so a colon is needed.

32. **C) is correct.** Subject and verb only agree in Choice C. In Choice A, *Garden* requires a singular verb (*offers*), as does *System* in Choice B (*is*). In Choice D, the subject *field* requires a singular verb (*is*).

33. **B) is correct.** Choice B is written in an academic style. Choice A discusses a topic that isn't relevant to a scientific paper. Choice C inappropriately uses the first person, and Choice D uses informal language (*really silly*).

34. **A) is correct.** The predicate includes the main verb of the sentence.

35. **D) is correct.** *Interupted* should be spelled *interrupted*.

36. **B) is correct.** *Enviornmentalists* should be spelled *environmentalists*.

37. **C) is correct.** *Normalized* best describes the idea the bats are now all the same shape, size, and weight.

38. **D) is correct.** *Each of which* is singular, so it requires the singular pronoun *its*.

39. **C) is correct.** The prefix *anti–* means *opposite* or *against*. *Fore–* means *before*, *bi–* means *two*, and *trans–* means *across*.

40. **B) is correct.** *Disrespectful* best describes the idea that the students were behaving rudely and deserved to be disciplined.

41. **C) is correct.** *Chron* is used in words relating to time (e.g., *chronology*, *synchronize*).

42. **D) is correct.** Here, a comma correctly sets off the introductory phrase;

furthermore, the sentence does not include an apostrophe in the pronoun *its*.

43. **A) is correct.** The first clause is dependent and the second is independent, so they should be joined by a comma.

44. **A) is correct.** *Improving* best conveys the idea described in the sentence that Esperanto was intended to enhance international communication.

45. **D) is correct.** Only Choice D includes a single independent clause with no other clauses.

46. **B) is correct.** The prefix *lexi–* means *related to words*.

47. **D) is correct.** An independent clause (*the fully…of Rome*) is connected with a dependent clause (*Although organized… Egyptian times*) using a comma.

48. **A) is correct.** The other choices all discuss the importance of the game to the town, so Choice A does not belong.

49. **C) is correct.** In the sentence, *handsome* is an adjective describing Narcissus.

50. **D) is correct.** In the sentence, *drag* is used as a slang term that means something is annoying or boring.

51. **A) is correct.** The comma is not needed to separate *such as* from the list it introduces. A comma is needed to separate items in a series (Choice B) and to set apart an introductory phrase (Choice C). The sentence does not convey emotion or ask a question, so a period (Choice D) is appropriate.

52. **A) is correct.** *Shelf* is correctly made plural as *shelves*. *Phenomenons* should be *phenomena*, *mans* should be *men*, and *deers* should be *deer*.

53. **B) is correct.** *Travels* functions as a noun and is the subject of the sentence.

54. **A) is correct.** A comma should never separate a subject (*Nile River*) from its verb (*passes*). Choice B correctly separates the dependent from the independent clause. Choice D correctly ends the sentence.

55. **D) is correct.** Only in this choice do the three phrases have a similar (parallel) structure (verb + direct object).

56. **C) is correct.** The outline shows that the First Stage of labor is broken down into three phases (Early, Active, and Transition).

WANT MORE?

Try our online *HESI A² Prep Course*

Dear Reader,

Here at Trivium Test Prep, we understand how important scoring well on the HESI A² exam is for your future. We believe you can never be "too prepared" for such a life-changing test. We are excited to offer you a comprehensive online course devoted to the HESI A²! Our ***HESI A² Prep Course*** includes:

- a <u>complete review</u> of all content on the HESI A² exam, with **trackable course progress** so you know exactly what you still need to review;
- <u>subject quizzes</u> at the end of each section, so you can **assess your retention** before moving on to new units;
- <u>two full practice exams</u> with **fully explained answer rationales** and **trackable scoring**, so you can measure your progress and understand what you need to improve on;
- and <u>full accessibility</u> via your computer, tablet, and mobile phone 24/7, enabling you to **learn at home or on-the-go!**

Best of all, our unique material and practice questions are available exclusively through ***HESI A² Prep Course***, ensuring you get double the study time when coupled with this book!

Trivium Test Prep's ***HESI A² Prep Course*** is available to current customers like you at the promotional price of only **$39.99!** Many less convenient programs retail for hundreds of dollars online. To enroll today and start learning immediately, please visit:

http://course.triviumtestprep.com/

Thank you for choosing Trivium Test Prep for all your HESI A² study needs! Best of luck with your studies,

— *The Trivium Test Prep Team*

Made in the USA
Las Vegas, NV
10 October 2022

56987637R00057